ALL ABOUT Grey and Grey Green Budgerigars

by

Roy Stringer

and

Fred Wright

First Published 1993

ISBN 0 9518145 4 0

Typeset in New Century Schoolbook and Printed in Britain by Spottiswoode Ballantyne, Colchester, Essex, England. Published by Roy Stringer Publications, Somerdale Cottage, Station Road, Westbury, Shropshire.

CONTENTS

Acknowledgements

Roy Stringer and Fred Wright gratefully acknowledge the kindness of Eric Peake in offering us the idea for this series of books and for painting the lovely Grey Budgerigar on the cover, the great effort put in by Les Lockey, himself a very successful champion breeder, exhibitor and judge of Budgerigars, in travelling around Britain and to Germany to take photographs of the experts, their birdrooms and - most importantly - their superb Grey and Grey Green Budgerigars specifically for this book, Harry Bryan, for delving into his wonderful memory to recall some outstanding Greys and Grey Greens from the past, Brian Byles, Editor of *Cage & Aviary Birds* and Peter Moss, Editor of *Bird keeper* for their support and advice during the book's preparation. Then, of course, there are the experts who have answered dozens of questions in our quest to discover what it is that has brought them success at the highest levels with Grey and Grey Green Budgerigars; Gordon and Sylvia Hallam, Bernard Kellett, Frank and John Punchard and Jo Mannes. We thank them all.

FOREWORD

by Eric Peake

When, in 1992, the first two books in this series were published one of my ambitions was fulfilled. For years I had contemplated writing such a series, dealing with different varieties and featuring the views of top breeders. When it became obvious that my painting commitments were pushing this prospect further into the future, I passed the idea to Roy Stringer and Fred Wright.

My belief that they would do the idea justice was amply justified by the excellence and popularity of *All About Greens* and *All About Red-eyes*. I was delighted to be asked to paint the covers for the books and to contribute the forewords, based on what I have observed when painting both the "Ideals" for several national societies and specific Budgerigars that have won major prizes. This, the third book in the series, deals with perhaps the most successful colour of all, the Grey Green, and its Blue series counterpart, the Grey.

Grey Greens have been bred to sizes beyond the belief of fanciers who have kept Budgerigars for many years. They seem to have dominated the specials at most leading shows. It is sometimes said that it is difficult to distinguish between the three colour groups of Grey Greens; light, medium and dark. I disagree. The light Grey Green has a mustard tinge to its base colour and silver-blue cheek patches. The medium Grey Green is more green than grey and its cheek patches are silver-grey. The dark Grey Green has a predominance of grey overlaying the green and its cheek patches are dark grey. The yellow of the face also varies with depth of colour.

The dark version seems to produce the largest birds but lacks the beauty of colour displayed by the other two. Some of the best Grey Greens produce chicks that have black beaks and claws. It would be interesting to research whether this has any bearing on the eventual size of the mature Budgerigar. Several studs of Grey Greens have impressed me over the years; in particular, the magnificent specimens bred by Tom Rothery and the bold-headed birds of the Pilkingtons.

Turning to Greys, I remember going to Southport in the mid-1950s and seeing a wonderful specimen exhibited by Harry Bryan. It looked like the painting of the "Ideal" brought to life. Another super Grey was Havenand & Ruthven's which took the best the best in show award at the Budgerigar Society Club show two years running.

Alf Ormerod, who bred some superb Greys, maintained that you had to be very careful when pairing Greys with Blues, to avoid creating a blue cast over the grey body colour. Care also has to be taken when using Opalines as outcrosses with Greys or Grey Greens. The danger is that body colour will show on the wings. One way of identifying a Grey or Grey Green is that its tail is black. On the best examples, all of the markings are deep black. Having read this book, I hope you will try to breed good examples of these very attractive varieties.

INTRODUCING GREYS and GREY GREENS

The story of the domesticated Budgerigar began when explorer, John Gould, brought the first pair to England in 1840. He had caught them on the Liverpool Plain of Southern Australia. Like every other wild Budgerigar, they were Greens – what we now call Light Greens. After about 30 years of Budgerigars breeding freely in captivity the first colour mutation appeared; the Light Yellow. Shortly afterwards the Blue and, after that, new colours seemed to appearing every few years with nine other colour mutations having been established before the Grey put in an appearance.

As so often happens with Budgerigar colour mutations, Greys appeared in more than one location, about the same time. It was around 1933 that breeders at the opposite ends of the world saw Grey Budgerigars for the first time; in Australia and England. However, this time they were not expressions of the same mutation. The Australian Grey was dominant to the existing colours, Light Green, Dark Green, Olive, Skyblue, Cobalt and Mauve (the Violet's appearance was still some three years off), whereas the English Grey was recessive. Put more simply, if you paired an Australian Grey to a Skyblue you would breed Greys in the first generation whereas with the English form it would take at least two generations and then only if the second year's pairing was appropriate.

Another difference soon became apparent. Australian Greys were bigger and bolder than English Greys and so the latter became neglected. Less than twenty-five years after their first appearance they were being reported as "extremely rare" and are now thought to have died out completely (perhaps during the Second World War when seed was virtually unobtainable in the UK and continental Europe) – though it is never possible to make such an assertion categorically when a recessive mutation is involved. There is always the possibility that, somewhere, there lurks a Budgerigar which carries the "lost" gene. It is only when two such birds come together that an English Grey would be bred and, even then, the chances are that it would be identified as an inferior Australian Grey! It would then almost certainly be discarded without breeding from it. Within a couple of years of its first appearance another expression of the Grey factor had been discovered. If you combined Grey with Green, a new colour, Grey Green was created.

It is better to think of Grey as a factor that can overlay an existing colour, rather than as a colour in its own right. So a Skyblue with a Grey factor added is a Light Grey. A Dark Green with a Grey factor added is a Medium

Grey Green. Indeed, until 1942, the Budgerigar Society's colour standards were still referring (far more accurately than today's terminology) to Grey Cobalts and Grey Mauves. So the Grey factor can make its presence felt in both colour series (Green and Blue) in all three shades (Light, Medium and Dark). When the Violet factor is added to the Medium Blue a particularly striking, warm coloration is created; sometimes mistaken for Mauve. Unlike the non-Grey forms, it is often not possible to distinguish between the three shades of Grey.

A fact that puzzles breeders who are not well-versed in the theory of genetics is that the Grey factor can be carried in single or double form – again not detectable by visual examination. This means that pairing a Grey to a Blue has several possible colour outcomes, depending upon whether the Grey is Light, Medium, Dark, single or double factor. If the Grey is a double factor you will produce all Greys (single-factor) and still not know what shade it is.

Assuming that the Grey is a single factor of Medium shade and its mate is a Cobalt you could get quite a surprise when their chicks begin to feather up. You could have Greys (of all three shades) plus Skyblues, Cobalts and Mauves. Take this a step further, by pairing a Grey with a Dark Green bred from a Blue (Dark Green/Blue), and you could finish up with any combination of Grey, Grey Green, Light Green, Dark Green, Olive, Skyblue, Cobalt and Mauve. Add to that the fact that Greys and Grey Greens tend to be big and bold – probably the strongest "colour" in present-day exhibition studs, often taking top prizes at major shows – and you will see that the Grey factor is not one to be dismissed lightly.

Grey and Grey Green Budgerigars are often maligned for their "lack of beauty". The person who makes such an accusation cannot have studied them very closely. Their coloration has a clean crispness lacking in some of their brighter counterparts and it is unusual to see a Grey or Grey Green with the patchy body colour regularly seen in "more beautiful" Blues.

When William Watmough wrote *The Cult of the Budgerigar* in 1935 he advised wide use of the Light Green to improve other mutations. He coined the term: "dipping into the Green" and typical of his advice was: ". . . my experience and the experience of others have proved that if season after season one persists in mating the more modern colours without any introduction of Green, type and size deteriorate . . ." Some 60 years later, many believe that it is Greys and Grey Greens that can improve every other variety, including Light Greens. If Mr Watmough was alive today, he could well be advising "dipping into the Grey".

The objective of the authors* of this book – and the other books in the *All about . . .* series – is to offer a platform for some of the world's most successful breeders of particular Budgerigar varieties to reveal their techniques, methods, likes, dislikes and hopes for the future. We believe we have succeeded. The experts have not been "led" when answering the comprehensive range of questions put to them and editing has been kept to a minimum. After studying their answers, readers may like to look for the reasons behind each expert's success.

You will not find the colour standards or scale of points of any organisation – for more than one reason. Different countries have different standards. There is a distinct possibility that an international standard could be agreed before the end of the century. If you want to read a particular club's standards you can join the club – the space in this book is better devoted to the opinions of the breeders who have proved their ability by winning at the very highest levels. Colour standards and points allocations vary, but an outstanding Budgerigar is recognised the world over.

**(Roy Stringer, formerly a design engineer in the motor industry, is Features Editor of CAGE & AVIARY BIRDS. Fred Wright, once a teacher, is now freelance avicultural consultant to several companies and a regular contributor of articles to the same weekly journal. Both are successful champion breeders and exhibitors of Budgerigars and international judges.)*

Harry Bryan looks back

■ *Harry Bryan is the most successful Budgerigar fancier the world has ever known. He began keeping Budgerigars in 1916 and, in 1993, is still enjoying success on the show bench. In the intervening years he saw all of the top Budgerigars in the UK which until recently, in Budgerigar terms, meant the world. His memory is as keen as ever and here he recalls names from the past and some from the present; the top breeders of Grey and Grey Green Budgerigars of their time.*

Grey Greens have been the most powerful of all the Budgerigar colours over the past 20 years. They carry more feather than the others and are an important colour to have in any fancier's stud, no matter what particular variety is being concentrated upon.

It may surprise some recent newcomers to the Fancy to learn that the first Grey Greens were not very striking; they were certainly no match for the Light Greens of the 1930s and 40s. Their strength was their ability to improve quickly. In my experience, it is not only in feather that Grey Greens hold a lead over the rest, the best examples are also big-boned.

The great step forward came when Joe Collyer, of Surrey, bred two wonder Grey Greens from an average pair; a Grey cock and a Green hen. In my experience they were the first Budgerigars to display wide faces. Maurice Finey bought one and Bill Addey the other. Shortly after he bought it, the one in Bill's possession became ill and he contacted me to see if I knew of any treatment that might save it. At the time, Bill had shown a lot of interest in a good Light Green cock that I had bred and so I took a gamble and swapped my Green for the sick Grey Green. I managed to return the Grey Green to fitness and it did a lot of winning and bred some really good chicks for me.

Another outstanding Grey Green to grace my stud was a cock bred by Jim Hutton. It came from Light Green cock he acquired from me and one of his good Spangle Grey Green hens. The pair produced 16 chicks and every one was a good one. A Grey cock from the same pair also won well for me. In his time, Alf Ormerod had some good Grey Greens and, coming even further up to date, three family partnerships, Gerald & Craig Binks, Terry & Clare Pilkington and Gordon & Sylvia Hallam, have bred some quite outstanding examples.

Grey is another powerful colour, if not quite as strong as the Grey Green. Amy Brown, of Croydon, bred an early one which she sold to Frank Waite. Shortly afterwards, I acquired a Grey youngster from Frank. As their exhibition quality improved, Ken Farmer had some really good Greys but he was never an enthusiastic exhibitor. Jack Fisher bred a wonder Grey cock but because it was late-bred it was never exhibited as a young bird. When

Jack died, the Grey came to me but it seemed to be an ill-fated bird. It flew into the wall of the flight and damaged its wing, so it was never shown at all.

Perhaps the best Budgerigar I have ever seen was a Grey cock; the one that took the top award at the Budgerigar Society Club Show two years running for Havenand & Ruthven. At the time I had a really outstanding Grey of my own which won 14 times out of 16 outings. On the two occasions it failed to win, it was beaten by Havenand & Ruthven's at the BS Club Show; once as a breeder and once as an adult. Mrs Angela Moss had some wonderful Greys and I must say that I am proud of some of the Greys that I bred over the years.

To reiterate, Greys and Grey Greens are powerful Budgerigar varieties. Like all other colours they have their good and bad years, but they are so strong that even if they do fall back from time to time you can be certain that they will come again.

("The Budgerigar Man", the Harry Bryan story and way of breeding exhibition Budgerigars is available from the publishers of this book)

MEET THE EXPERTS

GORDON and SYLVIA HALLAM are a husband and wife partnership who live in Worsley Village, by the side of the M62 motorway, a few miles north of Manchester, England. They bred Budgerigars for pets in the 1950s but moved on to breed exhibition Rabbits. After 20 years - and having won almost everything there was to win - they became disillusioned with the people in the Rabbit Fancy and looked for a new challenge. They decided to try Budgerigars for a second time; but this time for exhibition. Gordon and Sylvia's record has been phenomenal. Mention quality Grey Green Budgerigars and the name Hallam is never far away. In their own words they have been "quite successful" in winning the best in show award at 30 championship shows, including 10 area society championships. On no fewer than 30 occasions they have taken the award for best breeder in show at championship shows. Justly famous for the quality of their hens, the partners have taken best opposite sex awards on numerous occasions at top level shows, including Budgerigar World and the Budgerigar Society Club Show. By the end of the 1992 show season they had accumulated 230 Budgerigar Society best-of-colour challenge certificates; 100 of them with Normal Grey Greens and Greys. Budgerigars run in the family and son Peter, who lives nearby has made a name for himself by taking many top Budgerigar awards.

BERNARD KELLETT lives in Heaton Moor, a suburb of both Stockport and Manchester, in the north of England. It was in the early 1960s that he obtained his first Budgerigars. There were Grey Greens among them but they did not appeal to him any more than any other colour. It was simply a matter of purchasing the best birds that were available. Bernard has always been fascinated by the breeding aspect of keeping Budgerigars and he confesses to being a reluctant exhibitor though his showing activities were also limited by other factors. He had four children to rear, a stressful profession as a lecturer in Economics and a demanding hobby as a musician which took up a great deal of time at week-ends. He is in great demand as a lecturer both because of his deep knowledge of feathering – which after all is what the modern Budgerigar is about – and his skill as a speaker. More recently "the featherman" has devoted a lot of time to lectures and slide shows, judging and, when pressed, to exhibiting his high-quality Budgerigars. When he has exhibited he has won numerous Budgerigar Society challenge certificates. His first major win came in the early 1980s, at Bury BS championship show, when his breeder Grey cock took the best in show award. In 1987 he took best in show awards at Lancashire, Cheshire & North Wales BS (LC&NWBS) area championship and Budgerigar World with a Skyblue cock; the product of a Green x Grey pairing. His hens have taken several best opposite sex awards and in 1992 he took the best breeder in show award at the LC&NWBS area championship with a young Cinnamon Skyblue cock.

FRANK and JOHN PUNCHARD are a father and son partnership who reside in the rural part of Leicestershire, England. Frank lives in the heart of fox-hunting country and John some 10 miles away. Greys and Grey Greens were the best Budgerigars in the Punchard stud from the beginning in the 1950s; before John was dreamt about. When John joined the partnership in the early 1970s Greys and Grey Greens were already predominant but not yet of the high standard required to win major specials. The challenge of beating the best began and is still going on. The partners' first best in show at an area championship came at South Midlands B&FBS in 1978, with a young Grey Green cock. This cock and a cousin gained five best breeder awards between them. Over the years, more than 40 challenge certificates have been won with 15 different owner-bred Budgerigars and the most recent best-in-show came at Allestree & Derby, with a young Grey cock, and at Northampton BS with a different, adult Grey. A quirk of the stud is that the major wins have come with Budgerigars of different colours, produced from Greys and Grey Greens. A Cinnamon Light Green cock took nine CCs and five best in shows, including at the 1985 BS Convention. Two 1985 brothers, a Light Green and a Skyblue, won 15 best of colour and four best in show awards. At the BS Club Show, a Light Green cock gained fourth best adult, the adult CC and best Green in show in 1989. The following year a young Light Green hen took the awards for second best champion breeder, the young bird CC and best Normal Green or Grey Green breeder.

JO MANNES lives at Freiburg, in the Black Forest region of Germany. He has a high-class pet shop in the town which specialises in tropical fish. Jo was successful at exhibiting fish before reaching the top with Budgerigars. He is clearly a livestock man. It was in the late 1960s that he took up Budgerigars; starting with German stock. Then he began to visit the UK. At first he just studied the Budgerigars that appealed to him most. He recalls accompaning Reinhard Molkentin on a trip to the Ormerod & Sadler establishment, in the south of England, and sitting quietly with Doug Sadler, just considering the Budgerigars, while Reinhard was buying birds from Alf. When Jo began to buy stock, from such eminent breeders as Ormerod & Sadler, Ken Farmer and George Jenkins, he chose those which had feather growing outwards above the eye. On one of his trips he acquired a 1979 Grey Green cock which had been bred by Jim Moffat. That cock was paired with a Dominant Pied hen and Jo is convinced that the masks displayed by his stock owe their excellence to this pair. Most recent among Jo Mannes' many notable wins with Greys and Grey Greens have been: best young bird at Holland BS with a Grey cock in 1991; best in show with a Grey Green hen and best opposite sex with a Grey cock at Germany's AZ Club Show, also in 1991; best in show with a Grey cock and best opposite sex with a Grey Green hen at the 1992 European championship. At the same event in August 1993 he benched best in show and best young bird with a Light Green cock, best opposite sex with a Grey Green hen and best Grey Green with a cock.

CHAPTER 1

THEIR BIRDROOMS

Describe your birdroom.

Gordon and Sylvia Hallam:

We have five birdrooms, all of which were built to our specification by a local firm. They are all constructed from $\frac{3}{4}$ inch (18mm) tongue and groove boarding which runs vertically. Floors and roofs are made from 1in (25mm) thick marine ply. The internal walls and ceiling are lined with plyboard and the 2in (50mm) cavity created is filled with roof insulating material. The roofs are flat, built with a slope so that water runs off. The sheds are treated regularly with cedar-coloured *Cuprinol* and have a matured look. The first room built measures 16ft x 6ft (4.9m x 1.8m) and contains 24 cages, each measuring 24in x 18in x 18in (61cm x 46cm x46cm). These are mounted on the back wall so that they face the windows, which have a northern aspect. Removing cage dividers can create flight cages 4ft, 6ft or 8ft long (1.2m, 1.8m or 2.4m). Room No.2 is 12ft x 7ft (3.7m x 2.1m) and is utilised as an "L"-shaped internal flight. Room No.3 measures 10ft x 6ft (3.0m x 1.8m) and contains 15 cages, again 24in x 18in x 18in. The arrangement is the same as in room No.1 except that this time the windows face south and flight cages of up to 10ft in length can be created. Both rooms 4 and 5 are 9ft x 6ft (2.7m x 1.8m) and each contains 12 cages of the same proportions as those already mentioned. We do not have outside flights because of the problems of security, health risks and limitations of use. It is impossible to alarm an external flight completely and so, in this day and age, we feel it is not prudent to use them. Budgerigars in an outside flight can be contaminated by wild birds. At some times of the year outside flights can be used for only a few hours a day. With artificial lighting, an internal flight can be used for as long as you choose. All our cages are constructed from melamine-covered chipboard. All edges and the vertical cage supports are also protected by white plastic. This material makes it very easy to build cages; cleaning is easy and no maintainence is required. However, when cleaning, use only a damp cloth as excessive water might expand the chipboard. Cage dividers are made from semi-clear plastic. Having tried other designs we now use desk-type nest-boxes with the entrance hole in the top. These are placed inside the cage. Although no more productive than other types, we feel that they have a number of advantages. First, they are safer in that they cannot be disturbed by visitors to the birdroom brushing against them. Second, because the box is removed from the cage to be examined, the breeding pair has the opportunity to exercise and fraternise. Third, they make it easy to transfer a pair to another cage. The parents are

Gordon and Sylvia Hallam have five well-designed birdrooms set around their attractive garden. Four of them are equipped with cages as shown here (below).

chased into the box. A hand is placed over the entrance hole and the box and its contents are moved to the new cage. Each birdroom has its own *Sinderin* lighting control panel to give a gradual "dawn", to turn the lights on and off during the day according to outside conditions and to dim gradually to create a "sunset". During the hours of darkness a nightlight remains illuminated, at a predetermined level. Every room has a *Dimplex* thermostatically-controlled, oil-filled radiator and a fan-driven ioniser and air purifier.

Bernard Kellett:

The two legs of my "L"-shaped birdroom measure 26ft x 10ft (7.9m x 3.0m) and 9ft x 6ft (2.7m x 1.8m). It is constructed of 3in x 2in (7.6cm x 5.1cm) framing and clad on the outside with asbestos sheets and on the inside with ¼in (6mm) plywood. Trapped between is 3in fibre glass insulation. The floor is of concrete covered with vynil which has a strong felt underlay. The roof slopes from 7ft (2.1m) high at the front to 6ft at the rear. Natural ventilation is provided by louvred windows in the front wall and there is a ventilator in the lower part of the entrance door. Forced ventilation is provided by a window fan and roof fan for 12 hours each day. When needed, even more ventilation can be provided by leaving the entrance door open and closing a mesh safety door. When I had outside flights they tended to be under used and vulnerable to interlopers. So I now have five, raised interior flights, each measuring 6ft x 3ft (1.8m x 0.9m). These can be extended by the use of interconnecting doors but I have found the activity level to be higher in a 6ft x 3ft unit, particularly when coarse-feathered Budgerigars are involved. There are 48 breeding cages situated along the entire length of the rear wall, in four rows of 12. In the non-breeding season removal of slides can create 16ft (4.9m) long flight cages. The rest of the wall space is taken up by the five flights, two 4ft (1.2m) nursery cages, a sink unit and work bench. Single breeding cages measure 22in x 16in x 14in (56m x 41m x 36m) but I prefer to give each pair a double cage which is 44in (1.1m) long. Each cage is equipped with a stainless steel tray to facilitate cleaning. I use outside nest-boxes which measure 9in x 9in x 6in (23cm x 23cm x 15cm), constructed from ½in (12mm) plywood. Access for inspection purposes is via a hinged door for the top tier of cages and by way of a top lid for the rest. A range of 5ft (1.5m) long fluorescent tubes provides lighting and there are nightlights; all controlled by a dimmer unit. Heating is provided by 5ft long tubular heaters strategically arranged around the room and heat loss reduced by the fibre glass insulation. The two previously-mentioned electric fans and a radio are controlled by a timer and two ionisers operate for 24 hours a day. Water - hot and cold - is available within the room which greatly facilitates such tasks as cleaning utensils and soaking millet sprays and naked oats. Beneath the raised flights is storage for plastic bins containing seeds, softfood, nest-boxes, show cages and other birdroom equipment.

Bernard Kellett's establishment demonstrates that even a large birdroom can be an attractive addition to a garden. The interior layout (below) maintains the same high standard of design.

Frank and John Punchard:

Frank's measures 34ft x 8ft (10.4m x 2.5m) and John's 23ft x 10ft (7.0m x 3.0m). Both are timber-framed and fixed with *Rawlbolts* to concrete bases, with a damp course between. Frank's room is clad with exterior plywood and John's with Shiplap boards. Slightly-sloping flat roofs (Frank's corrugated clear acrylic sheeting and John's felt-covered tongue and groove) are equipped with roof lights. The interiors are lined with white, plastic-faced hardboard. John's is fully insulated with plastic sheets and 2in (5cm) thick polystyrene inserted behind the lining. Only John's room has a window in the front wall but both have ventilators mounted a little above floor level at one end and provision for extraction just below ceiling level, at the other. Access into the rooms is by door in the front wall. Supplies of water and electricity are routed underground. The layouts of the rooms are as follows. Frank's room has been divided into two. The main breeding room contains 27 breeding cages while the smaller room contains a block of eight cages and two flight cages. The larger room contains two inside flights (9ft 9in x 3ft 3in (3m x 1m)) with storage space beneath. The reduced height of these flights makes them ideal for Budgerigars that do not like large flights. The inside flights lead to outside flights of the same horizontal proportions but 6ft 6in (2m) high. Two smaller outside flights are accessed from flight cages and are used to house nest feather youngsters. John's room has 24 breeding cages on the back wall, a large inside flight (8ft x 6ft (2.4m x 1.8m)) and a smaller one (10ft x 4ft) from floor to ceiling. Both lead to a (11ft x 6ft (3.4m x 1.9m)) outside flight which converts quickly into two sections. The roofs of both partners' outside flights are covered to afford protection from the elements and predators. Their floors are covered with pebbles. Perching consists of dowelling; ranging in size from 12mm to 25mm. With the exception of 12 cages at Frank's, which are slightly smaller, all breeding cages are the same size and built as double-breeders with hardboard dividers. The cages measure 5ft x 1ft 4in x 1ft (152cm x 41cm x 31cm) and are constructed from 10mm exterior ply. Cage floors are painted with white gloss and the rest with a good-quality white emulsion. Punch-bar fronts have central doors and a small nest-box entry door at the top right-hand corner. Nest-boxes are 9in long x 9in high x 5in wide (23cm x 23cm x 13cm) constructed from 10mm ply. The outside end has two flaps (one hinged at the top and the other at the bottom); the top door for inspections and the bottom for replacing the concave. Both rooms have a similar level of equipment. Fluorescent tubes for lighting and small wattage filament bulbs for nightlights (controlled on separate time switches) and thermostatically-controlled electric heaters. Extractor fans are connected to time switches and, at John's, two ionisers work continuously. Electric water heaters are mounted above sinks which drain to soakaways.

Frank and John Punchard each maintain their own birdrooms. Here we see John's well-constructed room with its conventional interior layout.

Jo Mannes' large, block-built birdroom has a precast concrete roof incorporating opening roof lights. The interior view (below) shows some of the 100 breeding cages it contains.

Jo Mannes:

The overall size of my birdroom is 60ft by 20ft (18.3m x 6.1m). It is block-built and has a precast concrete roof with three 4ft square (1.2m x 1.2m) opening roof lights. The solid floor and walls are tiled. The structure is divided into a main room and a preparation area. In the main room are three large inside flights measuring 13ft x 10ft, 10ft x 10ft and 10ft x 7ft (4.0m x 3.0m, 3.0m x 3.0m, 3.0m x 2.1m). The flights have solid walls up to 3ft (91cm) high and then there is mesh mounted on welded and pop-riveted aluminium frames. This arrangement is easy to keep clean and cannot be damaged by the birds' gnawing. I have no space for outside flights but do not feel that my birds have suffered in any way by being housed inside. Buff Budgerigars need some protection from the weather and mine tend to be lazy. Having to cope with outside flights might not do some of them any good. From my point of view, it is easier to study my stock when they are all housed inside. In all, there are 100 breeding cages, each measuring 30in x 18in x 15in (80cm x 43cm x 37cm). They are constructed from 4mm thick aluminium-coated plastic sheets and the removal of patterned glass dividers creates five-cage-long stock cages. Each breeding cage is equipped with two perches; one round and one square. The cages do not have trays but their floors are covered with sawdust and white sand which is regularly replaced. I believe that Budgerigars will breed in any sort of box but, for my own convenience, I use the external, "box-within-a-box" type. They are 10in long x 6in wide x 10in high (25.4cm x 15.2cm x 25.4cm) and made of plywood. The level of equipment fits in with my requirements. It consists of electricity, kitchen units with hot and cold water, extractor fans, telephone, intercom to house, closed circuit television, radio and central heating from the house system.

Closed-circuit television is included in the hi-tech equipment of Jo Mannes' birdroom.

CHAPTER 2

MANAGEMENT

Describe a typical day's activity in your birdroom during the breeding season.

Gordon and Sylvia Hallam:

Since retiring, we are lucky to be able to take a more leisurely approach to looking after our birds. In the morning, during the breeding season, we spend around 90 minutes with the birds. We always follow a set routine. Sylvia checks every nest-box, any new eggs are marked and entered on the record cards that are kept in an index file. Similarly, every chick is handled and checked and any hatching, ringing or death is entered on the cards. If she is not completely satisfied with the behaviour of parents – for whatever reason – a note is made and the next time the boxes are checked if there has been no improvement, consideration is given to whether changes should be made. For example, if chicks are not coming on as well as those in other boxes, they will be moved – assuming that a suitable foster nest is available. If a chick is stunted during the first few weeks of its life it will never attain its full potential and a possible winner could have been lost. While Sylvia is attending to the nest-boxes, Gordon feeds, waters and – if needed – cleans up any copious droppings from beneath the perches. We always work together so that any problem that may arise can be discussed without delay. In the evening, the only nest-boxes that are inspected are those with chicks and those in which eggs are due to hatch.

Bernard Kellett:

The first task each morning is to make a general check-up of all the stock. Prior to my retirement this was all I had time for, but nowadays I follow this up with a nest-box inspection, watering and feeding softfood. During the afternoons – when most egg laying takes place – I prefer to keep out of the aviary all together. After tea, I devote a lot of time to a thorough nest-box inspection, ringing chicks, checking beaks, feet and rings to make sure they are clean, replenishing sawdust, where needed, and entering up records. The birds are then fed the basic seed mixture and a 3in (75mm) piece of millet spray. Finally I make a visual check of all the stock. Generally, the morning's work takes three-quarters of an hour and the evening's about one-and-a-half hours. At week-ends, the cage and flight trays are removed and cleaned. Utensils are washed, soaked in *Virkon S* or *Milton*, dried and replenished.

Frank and John Punchard:

We follow a system which evolved when John lived at home, before his marriage. The time switch is set to give the birds time to feed before the first visit of the day to the birdroom. John makes a general check to see that all is well. When chicks are due to hatch, a finger drawer of softfood is given to the appropriate pairs. All pairs with chicks are checked and fed softfood. Frank's first visit includes feeding softfood to all the birds. The main activity takes place in the evening between 6 and 7pm. Pairs with chicks are fed every evening and the rest every other evening. Water is renewed every other evening. John then gives softfood to all of the stock whereas Frank gives it only to the pairs with chicks. When feeding is done, the floor is swept. The final and most pleasing task is inspecting nest-boxes (every box is checked every day). In John's room, each egg is numbered and recorded on a card. Knowing the hatching date of an egg has resulted in a 90 per cent success rate at helping chicks out of the shell. Frank leaves Nature to take its own course. Not marking eggs has not been found to make any difference to rate of fertility, addling or hatching. Once a week, grit pots are replenished and more time is given to general management; assessing fitness for future pairings, re-pairing and keeping chicks reasonably tame. Cages and nest-boxes are cleaned when required and not to any strict routine. When chicks are about three weeks old, nest-boxes have some debris removed and clean wood shavings mixed with what remains. When the chicks have left the nest the box is cleaned quickly but thoroughly. Frank spreads cleaning jobs through the week during his many visits to the birdroom, but John usually cleans on Saturday or Sunday mornings. Finger drawers are washed every week, water fountains every fortnight and feeding pots every month.

Jo Mannes:

I am totally a Budgerigar man. They are almost my full-time job; days, evenings and week-ends. I start early by checking the flights, cages and nest-boxes. Once the first egg has been laid, I place a plastic, dummy egg (about the size of a Parrot's egg) alongside it. This serves several purposes. It helps to lift the hen from her own eggs, the extra ventilation helps to prevent dead-in-shell, it retains heat and helps to keep the hen's own eggs warm when she leaves the nest and also helps to prevent the weight of the hen and older youngsters from crushing newly-hatched chicks. Softfood is fed and I sweep the floor. My wife runs our shop and I usually join her for part of most mornings. On returning home, just after lunch, I spend the rest of the day in the birdroom - until around 10.30 or 11pm and even later in the breeding season. To begin the second session, I spray the floors with water and sweep them. All surfaces and feeding dishes are washed every day. The open water dishes in the flights are washed twice a day. As I work I am thinking. If you want to make progress you need always to be thinking about possible future

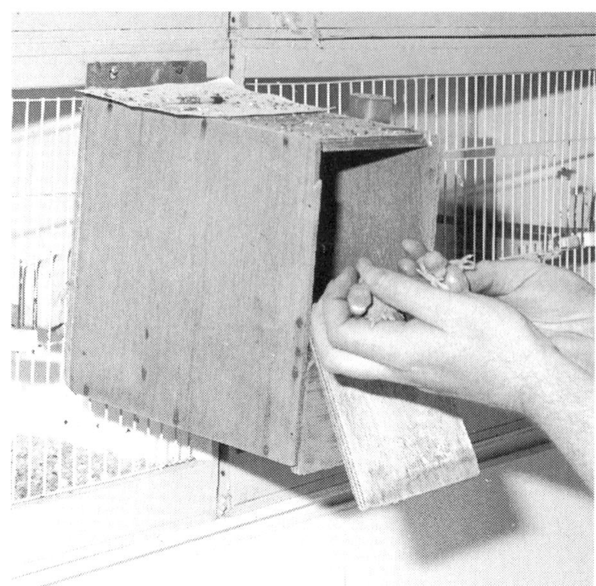

A handful of healthy chicks is a joy to hold - and behold. These are in the hands of John Punchard.

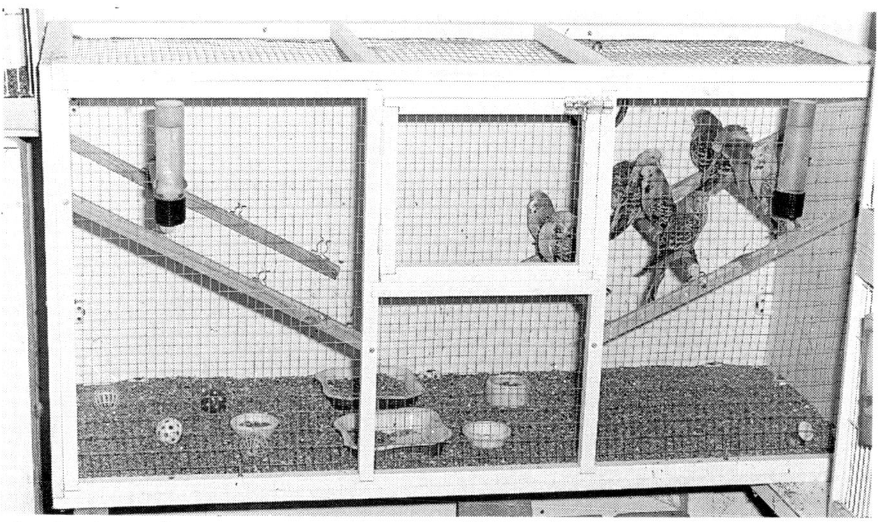

A wire-topped nursery cage gets young Budgerigars used to people moving around the birdroom. This one belongs to the Punchards.

pairings. I have to admit that I even think about pairings while driving. One of the biggest problems I have regarding working in the birdroom is the large number of fanciers who visit me. Keeping a room like mine clean is a constant task. I never allow the room to become dirty and there is far too much to be done for it to take just one day a week. Even so, Saturday is my big cleaning day and I prefer not to have visitors then.

Describe the activity in you birdroom during the lead up to a show.

Gordon and Sylvia Hallam:

We like to keep most of our youngsters in flight cages until after the show season, to keep an eye on them. They also remain steady. We used to put youngsters in the flight because they moult more quickly there. For some weeks before the first show, all potential exhibits are housed in colour groups of the same sex. This makes it easier to evaluate them and cuts down the amount of squabbling. We like to house about 10 birds in each 10ft (3.0m) long flight cage. From the time they are installed in this accommodation we spray them with plenty of cold water, about twice a week. Spraying is carried out in a very large, all-wire, Parrakeet cage. The constant handling involved helps to steady any unruly youngsters and the water soon conditions their feathers. About five days before each show, all likely birds are superficially de-spotted and any bloodied heads are cleaned. The final spray is given three days before the show. On the day before the show we decide which will be shown and these birds are given the final spotting out. Any heads that show signs of being dirty are cleaned with a very, very weak solution of *Vanodine V18.* Bent tails and flights are straightened by being dipped in boiling water. Priority is given to birds that are in condition. By condition, we do not mean that they have to be feather perfect. If that was so, we would rarely have a Budgerigar to show. But it DOES mean that the bird

Jo Mannes favours "box within a box" type nest-boxes. Unlike some designs, they ensure that eggs and chicks are well contained.

should be tight-feathered, bright-eyed and alert with most of its feather in place. If the best bird is not fit, it is not exhibited. Many a reserve has surprised us by taking a major award. If the show is a two-day affair, it is imperative that the birds are watered on the first day, after judging, but strange water may upset them, so we always give millet sprays which have been soaked in water for two days and a drinker containing water from our own supply. We believe that every exhibitor should use show cage covers - as we always do. The show hall is usually very warm and, after spending many hours in that environment, any Budgerigar is susceptible to catching a chill when leaving the hall, particularly if there is a breeze blowing. The covers also prevent fright from bright sunlight or street lighting. If you have your name on the cage covers, they might just prevent someone else picking up your birds at lifting time. Following every show, the cages are wiped inside and out with a solution of *Virkon S*. Perches are checked to ensure that are firmly fixed. Cages or fronts that need it are retouched with paint.

Bernard Kellett:

By the time the show season comes around the show team will have evolved, over a period of time. Constant observation of one's stock in the flights coupled with catching up of birds with show potential, from time to time, means that selection is almost automatic. Having a relatively small stud further simplifies the matter. In mid-June I prepare two sets of treble-breeder cages; one for cocks and one for hens. The birds are allowed to settle for a few days and then sprayed in groups of four; using a solution of one teaspoonful of borax powder to one pint of hot water. After spraying, I use a toothbrush to wash their heads (by brushing from the cere backwards) and feathers around the beak, again with borax in hot water. Thereafter, show team is sprayed with tepid or cold water (depending upon the weather) on alternate days: early in the day to ensure that the birds are dry before roosting. From experience (sometimes costly!) I have found that heavy spraying of coarser feathered Budgerigars is not desirable. Their feather covering is far less impervious than finer-feathered Budgerigars and heavy spraying penetrates to their skin and can lead to fatal results. If I feel that a Budgerigar is too wet, I wrap it in a towel for a few seconds before replacing it in the stock cage. On dull days, when the birds are slow to dry out, I place them in a cage equipped with an infra-red lamp for an hour or so. Some fanciers might wish to hasten the moult and improve feather condition in preparation for the show season. In my experience, two steps can be taken. One is to reduce the light level within the birdroom. The impression that days are shortening can be created by having the lights go off at 7 or 8pm instead of much later. This also reduces activitiy and promotes longer rest and sleep periods. Another way of hastening the moult is to lightly spray all stock, even those in the flights, to increase preening activity. I rarely pull out broken tail or flight feathers but I do remove feather stumps - particularly in the tail - if I feel they are impeding the growth of new feathers. Any removal has to be undertaken with great care because of possible damage to the feather follicle. In recent years there appears to have been an upsurge in the numbers of "tail-less wonders" and although this may be the result of inheritance or some form of latent French moult, it is possible that damage to the follicles contributes to the problem. The preparation changes during the week prior to the show. A very light spray is given for the first four days. This accelerates the birds' preening activity which increases the application of natural preening oil, so by the week-end the plumage carries a good sheen. On the Thursday I trim masks and on Friday I dip tails and main flight feathers in very hot water. This softens the feathers and makes it possible to straighten them. On cooling they stiffen into the correct shape.

Frank and John Punchard:

Youngsters are studied in the flight, as they moult. The adults' quality will already be known. A word of warning though, about assessing birds for showing while they are in the flights; many a "stormer" has turned into a shivering wreck when placed in a show cage. Sometimes it works the other way round. Show season work starts eight weeks before the first intended show. We catch up more birds to be prepared than we actually show. Any chewed up or broken feathers are removed and the birds returned to the flights. Only one tail feather is taken out at a time so that the remaining feather protects the growing one. The second is removed four weeks later, when the first one has partly regrown. Youngsters are caught up again six weeks before the show and adults two weeks later. They are housed in double breeder cages, with shavings on the floors, in groups of even numbers: the maximum being six. They are left to settle for four days before the daily show preparation routine begins. Feeding and watering is very much as during the breeding season. All show preparation is carried out at John's establishment, so spraying is done as soon as he gets in from work at 5.30pm. He would prefer to spray in the morning, but this is possible only at week-ends. Two birds at a time are placed in an old show cage which hangs above the sink. They are soaked by means of a large garden sprayer and returned to their stock cages. The lights are left on until 10.30pm to ensure that they are completely dry. Daily spraying continues up until the week of the show. It has been noticed that new feathers emerge about a week after spraying commences, so it is important to spray daily. Handling the show team every day gives an opportunity to check whether individual birds are putting on weight. If they do not, they are removed from the show team. Daily spraying continues until three days before the show, though some will be fitter than others when the final preparation is undertaken during the last week. If all the feathers are open, cold water is used in the sprayer. For Budgerigars with pin feathers, hot water is used. Closer to the show, the treatment is reduced to a fine spray to encourage preening which adds feather lustre. To avoid feather staining, iodine blocks are removed from the stock cages, perches are checked for cleanliness and the feeding of carrots is discontinued. De-spotting is carried out five or six days before the show to give the remaining feathers the chance of settling down. If bleeding occurs, cold water and a toothbrush are used to wash away the dried blood, always brushing in the direction of the feather growth. The bird is then sprayed. Frank prepares the show cages. Interiors are repainted and exteriors touched up before the show season starts. The cages are delivered to John the day before the show and seed is put in show cages and labels applied. A critical eye is cast over the team and if there is any doubt, the bird concerned is left at home. On the day of the show, the flights and tails of each member of the show team are dipped in very hot water to ensure they are straight. A hand is stroked several times through each bird's head feathers, from back to front, to make sure that any remaining feather sheath is removed.

Jo Mannes:

Budgerigars that are candidates for the show team are housed in 12ft long flight cages. At German shows it is important that both long tail feathers are in place so I pull all tails eight weeks before the show. First I cut the tail (which "kills" the feathers) and then pull them a week later. Using this method, I have never had the problem of tails failing to regrow. As an ongoing policy, broken flights are removed whenever I see them. At the beginning of the preparation period I house 10 to a cage but as the show approaches this number is reduced to four to give them plenty of space. If there are any signs of fighting the birds are moved around to achieve compatible groups. All mask spots are pulled five weeks before the show. My show team is sprayed, at first with warm water and later with cold, but not as often as is the case with some fanciers. A week before the show I wash heads and faces (and sometimes flights and tails) with warm water and baby shampoo. They are then rinsed with cold water. If any bird shows signs of moulting it is not sent to the show.

CHAPTER 3

FEEDING

How do you feed your Budgerigars?

Gordon and Sylvia Hallam:

Basic seed mixture:

Our basic mixture is *Beyers*' small Parrakeet from Belgium. This contains many seeds not normally given to Budgerigars, but our birds love it and we feel that offering such a wide variety covers most of their requirements.

Extras:

During the breeding season we give plain canary seed and groats, depending upon each particular pair's preference. If they like a lot of canary seed they can have it. If they do not, we give them only a little. Our principle is that if you offer Budgerigars what they like they will eat more of it and, in turn, feed more to their chicks. We never feed greenfood. It is almost impossible to ensure that greenfood has not been contaminated by chemicals or animals. When we kept Rabbits, our stock was known for constant good condition yet everyone except us fed greenfood. We do not believe it is essential for Budgerigars. We feed softfood prior to and during the breeding season. The content varies according to our fads, but the current formula is: a lightly scrambled egg (left to cool), mix in four tablespoons of *EMP* or *CEDE* egg food, one teaspoon of flaked wheatgerm and one tablespoon of pinhead oatmeal. This is extremely nutritious and eagerly eaten. Softfood is given in the morning so that none is left uneaten overnight. Millet sprays are given only as occasional treats, mainly to accustom show birds to them. The sprays are soaked for two days in water, strongly coloured with *Vanodine V18* and then well rinsed in fresh, clean water.

Drinking water:

After a gap of many years we have started to boil drinking water again. We felt that the quality of our domestic water supply had deteriorated and might adversely affect our birds. They seem to have benefited from the change. We have considered using bottled water but the expense and adverse reports on their contents have put us off. Bacteria breed freely in water, particularly when it contains vitamins and so every effort is made to keep drinking water clean. To avoid contamination, we give water in chinchilla drinkers which are stronger than those usually sold for Budgerigars.

Additives:

All through the breeding season, *Harkers Omnivit* is added to the water at the rate of half a measure to 2 pints (1.1 litres) of water: half the recommended strength. Non-breeding birds (in and out of the breeding season) receive *Omnivit* twice a month.

Grit and minerals:

We use *Caperns* grit which, though not cheap, is of superb quality and comprises very small pebbles which are unlikely to damage a bird's intestines. It also contains very little wasteful dust. *Liverine* Pigeon mineral blocks are always available. They are softer than the usual Budgerigar blocks but are much better value and, we believe, contain more minerals. The trick is to open the packets and to let them dry out for a few weeks before using them. Each brick is broken into four. We also give clean cuttlefish bone.

Bernard Kellett:

Basic seed mixture:

Each cage is furnished with an open dish containing *Trill*, which I have found to be a most reliable seed mixture. *Trill* have developed the mix and I believe they have got it right. On the outside of each cage are two *Flomatic* feeders, one containing Budgerigar tonic seed (refilled only once a week) and the other containing plain canary seed, during the breeding season only.

Extras:

During the breeding season, millet sprays which have been soaked overnight in a solution of *Virkon S* are given to each pair in 3in (75mm) pieces. A softfood mixture comprising 12 parts *EMP*, six parts *Baileys' No 1* horse meal and one part glucose powder is given in finger drawers. In the evening I give soaked naked oats mixed with grated carrot and a small amount of softfood. I feel that soaked seed is very important for youngsters which have just left the breeding cages because at this stage they are not drinking and the moisture content of the soaked seeds helps to compensate and prevent dehydration and loss of bodyweight.

Drinking water:

I give bottled natural spring water, all the year round, in plastic fountains fitted to the exteriors of cages and flights. In my part of the world the quality of tap water is too variable to give to Budgerigars

Additives:

At week-ends *Abidec* (3 drops per litre) and *Cytacon* (5mls per litre) are added to the drinking water. This continues all the year round. On the other five days I use *Lugol's* iodine at the rate recommended in an article written by Dr Walker. This has been very effective and disease and mortalities have decreased since its introduction.

Grit and minerals:

Some years ago my Budgerigars were suffering a lot of crop problems. Retford Laboratories informed me that the crop linings of birds which I submitted for post mortems were lacerated and susceptible to bacterial infection. On examination I found that my grit mixture contained a large proportion of oystershell which, when crushed, broke into razor-sharp discs. I immediately switched to *Caperns*' grit which is predominantly sandstone and, when crushed, forms tiny cobbles. Since that time I have had very few crop problems. I provide minerals and charcoal in finger drawers and iodine nibbles at all times. It is many years since I have used cuttlefish bone, which I discontinued because of pollution fears. Its omission has made no difference and I assume that the other minerals, etc. I feed satisfy my Budgerigars' calcium requirements. On the very few occasions that I have detected any signs of calcium deficiency (such as soft-shelled eggs) I add a few drops of *Sandoz Syrup* to the drinking water of the birds concerned; not to all the stock.

Frank and John Punchard:

Basic seed mixture:

Both partners feed *Versele-laga* Continental Budgerigar mixture (plain canary and peeled oats 7 per cent each, three oil seeds 9 per cent, safflower 3 per cent and the rest made up of three different millets). Birds can eat which seeds they require as their dietary needs change throughout the year. Frank adds Canadian plain canary seed; John adds Moroccan. John offer the seeds in separate dishes whereas Frank mixes equal quantities together. They agree that none of the mixtures they have tried has contained enough plain canary. John's Budgerigars' consumption of plain canary increases threefold once chicks are two weeks old. The odd pairs that do not increase its intake seem to produce backward chicks. Normally, neither would change their birds' diet halfway through the breeding season but, one year, John's pairs were not consuming plain canary and the chicks were of poor quality. He introduced *Haiths* Moroccan and results improved dramatically.

Extras:

Softfood is homemade and consists of: 1lb (0.45k) grated carrot, 3 slices wholemeal bread (dried in an oven until golden brown) and two large hard-boiled eggs. The eggs (complete with shells) are reduced in a blender and added to the grated carrot. The bread is crushed to crumbs and mixed in. A vitamin and mineral supplement (either *SA37* or *Stress*) is added - one teaspoonful for Frank's birds and two for John's. The mixture is fed in finger drawers, once a day to all breeding pairs and twice to those rearing chicks. A potful is put in the flight every day. Feeding softfood starts in October and continues until the end of the breeding season. John offered *Supafeed* the year round, when it was still available. Neither greenfood nor cuttlefish bone is offered due to the risk of contamination.

Drinking water:
Drinking water is offered in *Flomatic* drinkers. Frank's straight from the tap ("If it is good enough for me it will do the birds no harm." and after being passed through a charcoal-based filter by John ("I have seen the residue flushed out of water pipes!").

Additives:
Additives are no longer used in drinking water.

Grit and minerals:
Versel-laga mixed grit (containing redstone, corals and silicon) is always available in open pots; topped up every week and replaced every six weeks. John offers *Kilpatrick's* Pigeon Minerals the year round. To provide calcium for breeding hens, John adds one teaspoonful of calcium lactate and two of wheat germ oil to three pounds of seed, leaves it for 24 hours and mixes in another 3lbs (1.4k) of seed. This is fed over the same timescale as softfood.

Jo Mannes:

Basic seed mixture:
My basic seed mixture consists of 50 per cent plain canary, 20per cent white millet, 20 per cent Japanese millet, 5 per cent yellow millet and 5 per cent red millet. I formulated the mixture and it is marketed as "the Jo Mannes mix" by a leading European company. My birds consume 500 kilos (1,100 lbs) every eight weeks.

Extras:
I believe that feeding is one of the most important influences on the development of modern exhibition Budgerigars. Today's best Budgerigars cannot develop on a diet of only seed and water. Feather is protein and I boost my birds' protein intake with eggs. When the breeding season is in full swing I have about 90 pairs breeding and for these I boil 10 eggs every day. I mix the eggs with toasted bread in a food processor. To this I add soaked oats and a small amount of carrot and parsley. German-manufactured calcium and vitamin/mineral supplements are added to the softfood. All of my birds love this food and the way they feed their chicks on it has to be seen to be believed. The more chicks there are in the nest, the more of the softfood mixture they receive. I soak millet sprays for the breeding cages and flights. These have a soft seed and are easy for Budgerigars to eat. They take them in preference to the seed in the dishes. I believe that this feeding system brings out the full potential of my Budgerigars though, of course, it can only help create the right type of feathering if the potential is already in the breeding stock. I am a great believer in routine as far as Budgerigars are concerned. It is no good giving them extra food just at week-ends or at certain times of the year. My stud has received the same softfood mixture for 20 years. They need the same food every day.

A typical feeding station in a Jo Mannes' flight. The ceramic-tiled walls make the flights easy to clean.

Drinking water:

I add a soluble vitamin supplement to all of my Budgerigars' drinking water, at half the recommended strength to non-breeding birds. The water is boiled and then left to stand for 24 hours. Drinking water is changed every day; twice a day when the weather is hot.

Grit and Minerals:

A good quality mineral grit is available at all times. My Budgerigars also receive iodine/mineral blocks, cuttlefish bone and calcium powder in finger drawers. They also pick about in the sand which is placed on the flight and cage floors.

CHAPTER 4

MEDICATION

What do you look for when checking your birds' health and what do you do about it?

Gordon and Sylvia Hallam:

We are always on the alert for birds that are off colour. If spotted early enough, most birds recover quickly. With a little experience it is quite easy to spot birds that are not well. The main symptom is the "fluffed up" look. A Budgerigar that has its head under its wing and standing on two legs should be placed in isolation or with others in a similar condition. Sometimes it is a case of bullying. Budgerigars are natural bullies. Being moved to quieter quarters usually effects a rapid recovery. A few birds just do not like being kept in flights. Occasionally a bird will be seen to vomit or have a wet face and head. The vomit often has a vinegary smell. Since giving *Harkanker*, twice a year, as a preventative to trichmoniasis we rarely have this problem but an affected bird should be isolated. A course of *Harkanker* usually effects a cure. Another warning sign is a Budgerigar with a soiled back end – usually hens. We have found isolation and washing the soiled parts with a solution of *Virkon S* usually clears the problem. If not spotted quickly, soiling can become a complete blockage with death resulting. Birds that do not respond are dosed with cold tea for a week. This is followed by a five-day course of antibiotics, as prescribed by our vet. Any bird which looks ill and does not respond to treatment is put down. This is better than putting the rest of the stud at risk.

Bernard Kellett:

Daily inspection of all stock is high on my list of priorities because early treatment is essential when sickness occurs. Birds on the flight or cage floors, "fluffing up", dirty vents, sore eyes, wet masks and vomiting are the sort of symptoms I look for. In all cases, the first step is to separate a sick bird from the rest of the stock. Sick birds are a threat to the others and even in minor cases they are likely to be bullied. I have a home-made hospital cage fitted with an infra-red lamp. If a bird's vent is dirty or clogged it is vital to cleanse and sterilise this area to prevent re-infection occurring. Should medication be necessary – after separation and heat have failed – I administer terramycin mixed with warm milk and laced with *Abidec* to compensate for lack of food. This is given via a syringe directly into the crop

This homemade, wire-topped hospital cage, in Bernard Kellett's birdroom, has a heat lamp positioned above it so that a sick bird can choose whether to sit directly beneath its heat or to one side.

in serious cases or in a drinker in minor cases. Eye problems, which are more common in birds with directional feathering (head feathers which spread outwards as well as upwards), are treated by cutting away any encroaching feathers and applying eye drops or *Panalog*, depending upon the severity of the condition. For scaly face I use sulphur ointment or, for more persistent cases, *Ivomec*.

Frank and John Punchard:

The sooner an illness is detected the better, so it is essential to know the birds' individual characteristics and habits. Any change could be a sign of impending illness. It may only be an indication of the beginning of the moult, but it is better to be safe than sorry. Regular inspection of stock is essential. All birds, not only Budgerigars, are good at disguising illness so by the time a bird is seen sitting in the corner of the cage, it could be too late. The eye is good indicator of health. No matter what the feather condition, if a Budgerigar's eyes are bright it is in good health. Dull-eyed Budgerigars have something wrong with them, so we never use dull-eyed Budgerigars for breeding. A Budgerigar with droppings attached to the vent feathers ("clogged vent") will suffer only discomfort at first but the vent could become blocked; resulting in death. Any Budgerigar thought to be ill is isolated in a single breeding cage with fresh seed, softfood and water, but no grit. If it is seen eating it is merely left to build up its strength. If not, it is fed 2 to 3ml of glucose solution, five times a day, to maintain its strength. An infra-red dull emitter lamp is directed towards one corner of the cage so that the bird can move into its warmth or move away. We have no hospital cages. If, after 24 hours, there is no sign of improvement a 5 day course of antibiotics is started at the prescribed rate. If more than the odd bird becomes ill professional advice must be sought. For clogged vents, warm water and cotton wool are used to soak away the dried excreta and the bird isolated for a few days. Enteritis (green droppings) is a term used by fanciers to describe a symptom of many conditions.

Jo Mannes:

Anyone who has kept Budgerigars for even a short period of time can spot a Budgerigar that is fluffed-up and off-colour. I am always observing the flights and cages for signs of sickness. I have a quarantine room in the basement of my house and any sick bird is put into isolation there to avoid any risk of infecting the rest of the stud. The room is kept at 30 deg C and I have found that many Budgerigars recover if kept at that temperature for a few days. Any youngsters that may be afflicted by French moult are also removed to the quarantine room. If enteritis is detected, an antibiotic is administered. If there is no improvement after the course of treatment is completed the bird concerned is put down. Visitors often tell me about "wonder cures" for all Budgerigar ailments but I tend not to use them. I treat eye problems with a preparation which is produced to treat children's eye, ear and nose problems. Blocked nostrils are cleared with a pair of tweezers.

What does your birdroom's medicine chest contain?

Gordon and Sylvia Hallam:

Harkanker (Emtryl soluble), *Vanodine V18* (to clean and disinfect), *Virkon S* (a spray disinfectant), a wide-spectrum antibiotic, witch hazel (for swollen legs), strong nail clippers (to remove rings) and *Betsolan* (for inflamed eyes).

Bernard Kellett:

Terramycin, *Trykil* (Emtryl soluble), *Panalog*, sulphur ointment, eye drops, *Ivomec*, *Vanodine V18* and *Virkon S*.

Frank and John Punchard:

Optrex and *Betsolan* for eye complaints, a prescribed antibiotic (preferably terramycin), *Trykil* (Emtryl soluble) and *Levamisole.*

Jo Mannes:

Vanodine V18, eye medication, an antibiotic and a new antiseptic to treat bleeding (rather like *Vanodine* but red in colour). There are also many different, unused products given to me by friends.

Do you use medication on a routine, preventative basis?

Gordon and Sylvia Hallam:

All our Budgerigars are treated with Harkers *Harkanker* Soluble twice a year (against trichomoniasis); before and after the breeding season. Under no circumstances should this treatment be given DURING breeding activities as Budgerigars consume large quantities of water at that time and the results of ingesting more than the recommended dosage could prove fatal.

Bernard Kellett:

Twice a year I treat all birds with *Trykil* (against trichomoniasis), but on no account should this be given to breeding pairs because they drink far more water and would be fatally overdosed. Otherwise, medication is given only when needed. Providing Budgerigars are well fed, cleaned out regularly and their water renewed frequently disease is minimised. It is also important to avoid overcrowding.

Frank and John Punchard:

Trykil is administered (to prevent trichomoniasis) twice a year, one month prior to the intended pairing-up date and immediately after the breeding season. All the stock is wormed (using *Levamisole*) after the last show in September, with any new bird being treated as soon as it is introduced. Antibiotics are not given on a routine basis as their effectiveness might be impaired when they are really needed.

Jo Mannes:

My Budgerigars are given medication only when their condition requires it.

CHAPTER 5

THEIR STUDS

(Readers who are not conversant with the genetics of colour expectation will find it helpful to refer to Chapter 7 when the experts discuss pairings that produce Greys and Grey Greens).

How many Budgerigars do you keep and what varieties are they?

Gordon and Sylvia Hallam:

Prior to the breeding season we aim to retain around 180 Budgerigars made up of approximately 100 hens and 80 cocks. Although we use only 40 to 50 breeding cages, we like to have plenty of choice and plenty of reserves. It is far easier to sell good Budgerigars than to buy them. About 60 per cent of the stud are Grey Greens, 35 per cent Greys and the rest Greens. We prefer Normals but have a small number of Opalines, Cinnamons and Spangles – all in Grey Green, Grey or Light Green. We also keep a few Yellowface Greys.

Bernard Kellett:

Although I have room for around 300 Budgerigars, the maximum number I keep at any one time is 200. In the non-breeding season, after the surplus birds have been disposed of, numbers fall to less than 100. Of these, about 30 cocks and 45 hens are designated for the breeding team. The rest are spares, late-breds or older birds which have been retained for a variety of reasons. At least 75 per cent of my stock is Grey Green in Normal, Opaline and Cinnamon forms. The rest are Greys, Greens and Blues – all of which have descended from the Grey Greens. I recently brought in a few Spangles for outcrossing purposes; largely because it is so difficult to obtain high-quality Grey Greens.

Frank and John Punchard:

The stud is at its minimum just prior to the show season when Frank has about 80 Budgerigars and John about 100; with a 60/40 bias of hens to cocks. By the end of the breeding season it is hoped that there will be a combined total of 400. Greys and Grey Greens constitute around 60 per cent of Frank's stock and 70 per cent of John's. Frank had a very prolific Cinnamon cock of high quality a few years ago and so Cinnamons make up about 20 per cent of his stud. The rest are Light Greens, Skyblues, Dominant Pieds, Spangles and three pairs of Albinos. John would like there to be no non-Normal cocks in his stud but, at the time of writing, there are two. A number of Normal Cinnamon and Opaline hens are kept for their particular qualities. Normal Light Greens make up the vast majority of the rest of John's stud, with a few Skyblues and one or two Spangles and Yellowfaces. The Spangles, Dominant Pieds and Yellowfaces are all Normal versions of their varieties. Opaline Cinnamons are a rarity in either birdroom.

Jo Mannes:

Every year I breed between 600 and 800 youngsters and I believe in keeping plenty of adult Budgerigars; far more than most breeders. Many cock Budgerigars breed better in their second and third years. Indeed, I frequently do not even pair up a cock until it is two years old. Between 30 and 40 per cent of my stock is made up of Normal Greys and Grey Greens and then there are some Cinnamons and Opalines of the same colours. Only about 5 per cent of my stock is made up of Opalines and these are mainly hens that are used for the excellence of their mask spots. I keep all of the shades of Blues and Greens, including many Dark-factor birds both for their own value and because they can improve the coloration of the lighter shades. I also have Spangles, Dominant Pieds and a few Texas Clearbodies.

Which of the other varieties can improve your Greys and Grey Greens?

Gordon and Sylvia Hallam:

We do not keep any variety to boost another. Each one has to be strong enough to stand on its own. If it is not; it has to go. We want to breed good Budgerigars. Colour is not the prime consideration; quality is! But over the years, we have found that the Grey Green family is the strongest, with the Grey a close second. This is why our stud is dominated by these colours.

Bernard Kellett:

The varieties I have used to maintain or improve the quality of my Grey Greens have been Light Greens, Opalines and Cinnamons. I have found that Light Greens tend to produce a vivid and vibrant shade of Grey Green. By contrast, Blues and Greys tend to produce a duller shade. Opalines have been extremely useful in improving shoulder and mask qualities. The improvements have been even greater when the Opalines concerned have been slightly flecked which, although a fault, so often appears to be linked with coarser feathering. The influence of the Cinnamon input has been to bring style and balance to the Grey Greens. However, colour is only one consideration. Of equal importance are feather texture, feather length and skeletal properties. Thus, other varieties have been used to improve my Grey Greens only when they have excelled in these factors.

Frank and John Punchard:

Rather than "improving" Greys and Grey Greens, we think in terms of "refining" them. Normal Cinnamons help the feather texture, because many of our Greys and Grey Greens are rough feathered. Our Opalines are large spotted (and often flecked) which keeps the right level of melanin in the Normals to combat the opalescent effect seen around the necks of some Normals. In the past, Light Greens have been the most beneficial supplement as far as show birds are concerned. Their use has increased the number of single-factor Greys and Grey Greens which, in turn, has dramatically increased the number of show specimens when they have been paired together or back to Light Greens. In fact, most of our best Budgerigars have come from the following matings: single-factor Grey or Grey Green with single-factor Grey or Grey Green; single-factor Grey or Grey Green with Light Green/Blue. Double-factor Greys and Grey Greens produce mainly large, coarse-feathered birds which are used for breeding purposes only.

Jo Mannes:

Blues and Greens are very useful when breeding for Greys and Grey Greens. When you pair Blues or Greens with Greys or Grey Greens you produce only single-factor Greys and Grey Greens, which I prefer. By introducing Dark-factor birds, such as Cobalts and Dark Greens, you can increase the richness of colour of even Greys and Grey Greens. Spangles are very useful for keeping body colour bright.

CHAPTER 6

ALL ABOUT GREYS AND GREY GREENS

What is the attraction of Greys and Grey Greens and is specialising a good idea?

Gordon and Sylvia Hallam:

We did not set out to breed Grey Greens. Indeed our favourite colour was Light Green and ours was predominantly a Light Green stud until the late 1970s. It is true to say that our Grey Greens simply "evolved". Probably, the biggest influence in the evolution was our friendship with the late Harry Makinson who had a wonderful stud of Grey Greens in the early 1970s. Although we bought mainly Light Greens (which were a by-product for him) we did get a very inferior Grey Green which was superbly bred. This bird produced a number of good stock Budgerigars which, in turn, bred quite a few very high-quality Grey Greens. We have always believed in quality irrespective of colour and, inevitably, over a period of years our stud became dominated by the Grey factor; so much so that we rarely breed more than a handful of Light Greens each year. In our experience, Budgerigars with the Grey factor tend to be larger, with better head qualities. We shall continue to have a stud dominated by the Grey factor until the quality of another group directs us into other channels. Our aim is quite simply, quality. We want a stud that can hold its own on the show bench with the best. Specialisation is a good idea in most varieties. The more you breed of a particular colour, the more choice you will have and a greater ability to compete on equal or better terms with breeders of that variety who keep a mixture of colours. However, because some breeders specialise in a colour, they dispose of high quality Budgerigars of other colours. Likewise, when purchasing, they reject good birds because they are not of the colour in which they specialise. Had we followed that pathway, we believe that we would never have achieved many of our successes.

Bernard Kellett:

My primary objective in breeding Budgerigars is the production of a stud of birds that conforms with the "Ideal". This consideration transcends all others, including colour, and foolish would be the fancier who disposed of high-quality stock just because it was not his favourite colour.

Good stockmanship depends upon good observation. Here, Bernard Kellett studies the occupants of an inside flight.

The Grey Greens I have bred over the years have tended to be closer to the "Ideal" than other colours and it is for this reason that I tend to specialise. However, if I produce a quality bird of a different colour I retain it and use it to breed Grey Greens. One of the main attractions of the Grey Green, apart from its colour, is that it contains two colour elements, Grey and Green. This makes it easier to submerge and assimilate into the stud other colours, such as Blue. This makes specialisation a little easier. One fact that makes specialising in Grey Greens a challenge is that so many good fanciers breed and win with them. I have stuck at the task largely because of the consistency of quality of my family of Grey Greens over the last 20 years. It originated mainly from the Finey "Collier" strain which created such an impact many years ago and sentiment has played some part in my wanting to keep the line going. My targets are to build upon the work of the able fanciers who did so much to bring Grey Greens to prominence and to breed sufficient quality Budgerigars to make an impact within the Fancy. Specialisation in any variety has certain advantages, providing it is not specialisation to such an extent that other varieties and colours are excluded. I would prefer to be a specialist in Budgerigars of super quality than a specialist in one colour of mediocre quality. Harry Bryan and Alf Ormerod are good examples of fanciers with this attitude. A major advantage of specialising in Grey Greens is that other colours are produced and one can also enter Greens, Blues and Greys at shows. Specialisation makes it possible to enter several birds in the same class and there are always reserves available if one of the show team has to drop out. Specialising in one colour keeps a fancier "on the rails" in that he develops an eye for the variety and is often able to identify and concentrate the finer points which gives him a distinct advantage.

Frank and John Punchard:

The best Budgerigars that Frank bought, initially, were Greys and Grey Greens. These bred the best chicks and so what started out as a multi-variety stud gradually changed to one which was predominantly made up of Greys and Grey Greens. This was the situation when John became a partner and it was natural to continue what had already been started. Greys and Grey Greens generate a great amount of competition within their own classes and winning a class of Greys or Grey Greens is acknowledged as an achievement. Proportionally, their classes contain more high-quality Budgerigars than those for other colours. The fact that the Grey factor is dominant means that they produce Budgerigars of their own kind and could be expected to produce more good Budgerigars. The challenge is to upgrade the stud continually and when this is accomplished it can only be a matter of time before success is achieved. As you are able to pair up more, good Budgerigars in time the best that you produce will start to approach the Budgerigar Society's Ideal. In the broadest sense, every Budgerigar breeder specialises to some degree. Some just want to breed good Budgerigars. Others break this down further and choose a particular variety and others go further still and specialise in a colour of a variety. Specialising for us consists of keeping Normals, with the emphasis on Greys and Grey Greens. If an excellent Budgerigar of another variety was bred, we would retain it for our breeding team and try to breed better Normals from it. The advantages come from being able to prepare several birds of the same colour and sex, for show. Another advantage of specialising in Greys and Grey Greens is that, being dominant, they produce more Greys and Grey Greens no matter what you pair them with. A disadvantage of keeping a Normal stud is that a number of the birds will be split for sex-linked and recessive factors and these will appear when you do not want them.

Jo Mannes:

When I began buying stock from the UK, I bought very high-quality Budgerigars and several of them were Greys or Grey Greens. Grey is a factor which can be added to all of the other colours, rather than a colour in its own right. Because it can be carried as a single factor it means that the other colours remain readily accessible. The combination of Grey and Green, which gives us the Grey Green, tends to bring thicker feathering. This texture is very useful when breeding exhibition Budgerigars. I want to maintain the best stud in the world and to improve exhibition Budgerigars even further by extending the feathering on face and cap while keeping the body feathering tidy. Greys and Grey Greens will play a big part in helping me to do this. As far as specialisation is concerned, it is certainly a good idea to specialise – in good Budgerigars. The group of colours that make up Normals are compatible with each other and the standard of Normals is extremely high, so I can understand anyone wanting to specialise in Normals. I would not be happy specialising in only Greys and Grey Greens because this would involve breeding a high proportion of double-factor birds and this, in turn, would limit the number of Greens and Blues that are bred.

What makes a good – and a bad – Grey and Grey Green?

Gordon and Sylvia Hallam:

A good Grey or Grey Green is a good Budgerigar and some experienced fanciers can spot a good Budgerigar without analysing why it is good. It is this "eye" that all breeders should try to develop. The first features that catch the attention are type and size. A truly good Budgerigar should have a proud, almost haughty, look with a high, domed head. On closer examination it must have a wide face, with plenty of brow over the eyes and good frontal rise. A narrow face exaggerates browiness and sometimes fools judges, but it is folly to build a stud on narrow-faced winners. All quality exhibition Budgerigars should have some degree of brow. A good Budgerigar should have a good mask that commences well behind the eye and extends well below the beak. Many Budgerigars with good lower masks fail on upper mask because this commences in front of the eye. Apart from being a major fault it gives the appearance of a smaller face. The lower mask should be adorned with six, equally-spaced, round spots; the outer two being partially covered by the cheek flashes. The main fault here is badly shaped spots. In the quest for larger and larger spots many breeders ignore their roundness and very few of today's winners have well-shaped spots. It is impossible to get very large round spots unless the width of feather is exceptional. It is better to draw back a little on spot size to achieve better shape and, at the same time, you will tend to produce Budgerigars with less head flecking. Lack of width in the mask is another common failing. A wide mask gives the illusion of a bigger, more powerful face. But to attain that width you must have thickness of neck and shoulder. Backline is probably where most good Budgerigars fail. Really good width of neck and shoulder can produce a slight bump on the back of the neck. A slight raising of the rump feathers is also a possibility and many coarse-feathered Budgerigars have difficulty holding their tails in line with their backline. The perfect Budgerigar has yet to be seen and you must be aware of all faults if you are to make progress. In our opinion the worst faults are: 1) Hinged tail, 2) narrow face and head, 3) poor type/stance/backline, 4) flecking, 5) lack of head quality, 6) short and narrow masks, 7) lack of shoulder and thickness, 8) protruding beaks, 9) poor wing carriage, 10) short behind the perch and 11) badly-shaped spots.

Bernard Kellett:

A good Grey Green has the following attributes:
BOLDNESS. This is evident initially in the strength of its shoulders. Broad shoulders offer a foundation for a good, wide mask with uncluttered, well-shaped spots and a wide, flat-fronted face, beneath excellent frontal lift and backed by substantial backskull.
LENGTH. In recent years, so much concentration has been on head qualities that breeders have been producing short, cobby Budgerigars which are unbalanced and, very often, poor breeders. It is essential to maintain length behind the perch as well as in front.
COLOUR. A good Grey Green has a vibrant colour and should not be dull or insipid. Neither should it display opalescent markings.
CARRIAGE. A Budgerigar must be capable of showing off its superior qualities. The backline must be nearly straight and maintained to the end of the tail. It must stand at the correct angle and lift its body off the perch.
FEATHERS. Intermediate feathering is perhaps the most desirable quality of a show Budgerigar; backed by depth of mask and linear feathering around the eyes.
A poor Grey Green is one that fails to match up to the above characteristics viz: narrow shoulders and face, tight mask with spots almost touching each other, small or misshaped spots, split mask, poor backskull, no frontal rise, shortness of body, poor stance (including hinged tail, dropped or drooping wings) and drab colour.

Frank and John Punchard:

Greys and Grey Greens are no different from any other Budgerigar variety in that they should be as near to the Budgerigar Society's Ideal standard as possible. A good example should be bold and stand off the perch at an angle of 30 deg to the vertical. It should have a thick neck when viewed from any angle and with this comes a wide mask and width above, which are essential. A good set of feathers is required. This will make or break a bird, no matter how good its framework. The ideal feather type should be between the fine yellow and the coarse buff, with a slight tendency towards the buff. The overall effect should be silky without appearing coarse but still retaining the length and width which creates a deep mask. Because Greys and Grey Greens are among the duller colours, clear definition between the black markings and yellow or white background is essential. Black stands out more distinctly because the body colour is not commanding your attention; so well-defined markings are an advantage. Faults of size, shape and deportment apply to all varieties with the only specific faults of Greys and Grey Greens relating to their colour and markings. General faults are listed in order of personal dislike: lack of shoulder width (which leads to narrow masks and heads); lack of balance (this can show up in many ways such as a small head on a large body, a large head on a small body, long flights, long or dropped tail, in fact any feature which upsets a Budgerigar's deportment – having said that, a well-balanced, large Budgerigar will always beat a well-balanced, smaller one); short mask (where the spots are almost in line with the cheek flashes); lack of feather (this causes an otherwise excellent Budgerigar to become an also-ran). As far as colour and marking faults are concerned, the worst by far is opalescence around the neck. Wishy-washy, body colour and lack of definition of markings are on the increase.

Jo Mannes:

Just how good (or bad) an exhibition Budgerigar is depends upon its feathering – and that applies to all varieties including Greys and Grey Greens. A good Budgerigar is a big bird with wide, soft feathering; broad shoulders and a good spread of mask; directional feathering on the head to give an abundance of capping over the eyes; round spots; a small, tucked-in beak and rich, even colour. When I first went to the UK I saw lots of Buff-feathered Budgerigars there, but they were hard-feathered Buffs. I knew right from the start that what I wanted to breed was soft-feathered Buffs. Soft-feathered Buffs carry thick, wide feathering and this means that they carry round mask spots; a feature that can make the difference between winning and losing when two Budgerigars are very closely matched. A great advantage of soft-feathered Buffs is that they are far more fertile than their hard-feathered counterparts. I also divide Buff feathering into three further categories; short-feathered Buff, middle-Buff and super-Buff. To produce an absolutely outstanding exhibition Budgerigar we need to have a variation of feathering on the same bird; extra length and width on the head (to give the directional feathering which widens the head and mask) and shorter feathering on the body (to maintain neatness of outline). Very serious faults are: dropped tail; a short, tight mask; the combination of head flecking and small spots. In the final analysis, a bad Budgerigar is one that does not match the description of a good one.

Which faults are correctable and which are not?

Gordon and Sylvia Hallam:

All faults are correctable, but some faults are easier to correct than others. So much depends on the background of the Budgerigar in question. Whatever the fault, if it has not been seen in the background (ancestors) of the Budgerigar for some time, we would not expect the fault to be reproduced to any great extent – as long as it is paired with one that is free from the fault in all respects.

Bernard Kellett:

I have yet to see a Budgerigar which is completely faultless and correctability of any fault is dependent upon how much time one is prepared to spend – and how much risk is involved. For example, small spots are a fault that can easily be corrected; with little risk of spreading the fault throughout the stud. By contrast, a hinged tail is a major fault which may well prove insurmountable even over a long period – and there is a grave danger of spreading it through the stud. The general rule for cancelling out defects is to pair the Budgerigar with the fault to birds which excel in excellence for the same feature. Thus, for a small-spotted bird one would choose a large-spotted partner; provided that the former is strong in all other characteristics. The problem with balancing up pairings is that the bird with the fault may turn out to be more dominant than its partner. I prefer to double up on good features. Fortunately I have several friends who have had birds from me in the past and this means I can obtain a partially-related outcross.

Frank and John Punchard:

Every Budgerigar has faults, so it is a matter of weighing up its good points against its bad and deciding whether it is worth using it. If any fault is found to be carried in a dominant, hereditary form the whole family is disposed of. Describing all faults and explaining how to correct them would take a book in itself, but the general rule is not to double up on the same fault. To take an obvious example, if an otherwise excellent Budgerigar has pin-head-sized spots it should be paired with a good all-round mate which excels in spot size and shape. All faults are correctable. It is all a matter of selective breeding and retaining the young that have most desirable features.

Jo Mannes:

Every fault is correctable, though some are more difficult to correct than others. Small spots, for example can easily be improved by careful selection of pairings. However, there is more to mask spots than just their size. I like to see a round spot with a border of white or yellow all around the spot on each feather, including below. To achieve this the feathering needs to be wide and soft. If the feathering is hard the spots are likely to be long and pointed. Flecked Budgerigars should only be used if there is a very good reason for doing so. Like opalistic markings, flecking needs to be eliminated. In my view, opalescence is a serious fault in Normals and my experience suggests that it often comes from pairing Light Green to Light Green and Skyblue to Skyblue. The solution is to pair Greens and Blues with Greys and Grey Greens. This has the second benefit of reducing the number of double-factor Greys and Grey Greens that are produced. If both sides of the majority of pairings contained the Grey factor it would not be long before there were very few Light Greens and Skyblues in a stud. Opalines DO have a place in a Normal stud both for improving spot size and broadening the shoulders. Broad shoulders bring wide masks which permit better positioning of spots. If a fancier finds it necessary to breed with Budgerigars that have major faults, he should do it with great care. My stud is now so well established that there is no place in it for Budgerigars with major faults. My own solution to the problem of correcting faults is not to breed with any Budgerigar that displays them.

What do you think are the strengths of your own stud? Are there any features that you would like to improve? What do you think of other breeders' and other countries' Greys and Grey Greens?

Gordon and Sylvia Hallam:

We have been told by many fanciers that the strength of our stud is in its depth of quality. We are particularly strong with our hens. We may not have the best Grey Greens in the world, but we do have large numbers of quality birds with very few poor specimens. There are many fanciers who we admire for breeding good quality Budgerigars but few have consistently produced winners over a long period. Many have sprung onto the scene with a grand flourish only to disappear a few years later. The ones who succeed over a period of time are those who are determined and prepared to devote a great deal of time and effort. The percentage of man/wife partnerships that do well is above average, probably due partly to the extra time and effort they put in and to the support they are able to give each other. In recent years we have seen many photographs and reports of the high quality of overseas' Budgerigars and it may well be that if we ever see them on the show bench we will be in for an unpleasant shock. On the other hand, it is some comfort that overseas fanciers still come to the UK seeking to improve their studs. We believe that the overall quality of Budgerigars is higher now than it has ever been. In our twenty-odd years in the Fancy we have seen an improvement and a great levelling out. No longer is the Fancy dominated by a few "top-of-the-tree" champion names. Quality Budgerigars are distributed among many fanciers, in most sections. Honours are now spread widely, which is good for the Fancy.

Bernard Kellett:

The strongest feature in my stud is "face". In general my Budgerigars have width, good frontal rise and deep masks. The features I would like to improve upon are length of body above and below the perch and overall fertility. I admire the Budgerigars of several fanciers. Perhaps the

This lovely Grey Green demonstrates once again why Gordon and Sylvia Hallam are so well known for the quality of their hens.

best stud of Grey Greens I ever saw was the late Harry Makinson's, in Yorkshire. The best individual Grey Green I ever saw was one bred by the Ormerod & Sadler partnership, some years ago. In Lancashire, several breeders have produced exceptional Grey Greens in recent years. The Pilkingtons and the Hallams, in particular, have been very consistent over the last 10 years. Jim Moffat's and John Woods' studs have always impressed me greatly, although their Budgerigars are mainly Greens. Gerald and Craig Binks had an exceptionally good family of Grey Greens as has Charlie Bowman. My only first-hand experience of Budgerigars in other countries has been in the USA and Denmark. In America there are several outstanding studs but the best of the ones I have seen belong to Don Langell, Joe Sabella and the Lalavees. Each of these studs was well up to UK standards. When judging in Denmark I saw several top-class Budgerigars which had been bred from British stock. The Budgerigars of Jo Mannes are really excellent. This judgement is based upon the Mannes birds I have seen in the UK, video tapes and the reports of British fanciers who have visited him. At the time of writing, the Mannes stud is attracting a great deal of attention and fanciers from all over the world are flocking to see his Budgerigars, which have superb head and facial qualities. Their feathering appears to be extra long and almost silk-like to the touch. It is probable that this is the result of a new feather mutation and it will be fascinating to observe its impact on future generations of Budgerigars. As a rule, new mutations appear in several parts of the world within a short space of time. The rest of us can live in hope! However, overseas' studs tend to be multi-coloured and, although I have seen good, individual Grey Greens, I have yet to see a true specialist. Memory is one of Nature's great deceivers. I have frequently carried the vision of an outstanding Budgerigar of yesteryear only to find my idealism shattered when its photograph has been published, many years later. I can still see those rows of excellent Normals at Maurice Finey's, the fabulous Grey Greens of Harry Makinson and the outstanding specimens bred by Harry Bryan, Alf Ormerod and Mrs Angela Moss. These people stood out from the contemporaries because of their ability to produce outstanding Budgerigars consistently. Nowadays there appears to be a much more even distribution of quality.

Frank and John Punchard:

The strength of our stud is that we can reproduce its strong points in all our pairings and can improve on weaker points by introducing outcrosses – without destroying the strong points. Our specific strong points are: width of shoulder both in profile and front view, width and depth of mask; large frames and plenty of feather. We would like to improve showmanship. A lot of our Budgerigars sit at the correct angle but do not "blow" their top ends or stand clear of the perch. This ability can make an average Budgerigar look good. Lack of it can make a good Budgerigar look ordinary. For a number of years we have been improving "eyebrows"; trying to get the feathers that make up the cap between the cere and the eyes to grow horizontally rather than vertically. We both admire fanciers who can breed winners year after year. That brings the name of Harry Bryan to mind. But for his untimely death, Jack Fisher would have done the same. Since those days, although many fanciers have produced winners year after year, none has dominated the Fancy. The best Budgerigars are now more widely spread, which must be good for the hobby. Greys and Grey Greens are the backbone of the Fancy and the greatest depth of quality can be found in Britain. Certain studs from abroad have received a lot of exposure in the Fancy press and they certainly have superb studs. However, they tend to be the exception rather than the rule. On several trips to Europe, John saw the greatest quality in Germany, but the standard fell off quickly below champion status. With the exception of Jo Mannes' stud, the number of

Budgerigars capable of winning classes at the BS Club Show are small, however the quality is rising steadily. Of all the varieties, Greys and Grey Greens have achieved most success at the BS Club Show in the last 15 years, with seven best in shows or best breeder in shows. Particular Budgerigars that stick in our minds are: Havenand & Ruthven's double BS Club Show winning Grey cock of 1980 and 81, Barry Wilde's superb young Grey Green hen that won the Club Show in 1983, Les Lockey's Grey cock of the early 1980s that won everything except the BS Club Show (it was not shown there), Gerald and Craig Binks' 1987 Grey Green cock which was best breeders and, subsequently, took the second and third best adult awards at the Club Show and, finally, Gordon and Sylvia Hallam's Grey Green hen which was best opposite sex at the BS Club Show while still a baby.

Jo Mannes:

I believe that a great feature of my stud is that it is large and another is that it is made up mainly of Normals. For the rest, I can only quote the comments of other fanciers. It has been said and written that my stud: 1) has fantastic quality of feather; wide and soft; 2) is notable for the amount of directional head feathering, which gives capping; 3) has quality in depth in all of the main colours; 4) is very fertile and 5) has excellent depth of colour. I would like to increase the capping still further and am pleased to say that this feature has improved significantly over the last couple of years. It has been suggested that the type of feathering carried by my Budgerigars is the result of a mutation. I tend to think it is not. My initial aim was to put Cinnamon-type feathering on Normals. To this end I used Cinnamon hens and split Cinnamon cocks. It was at that stage that the "Mannes" feather was manufactured, rather than mutated. It is conceivable that a mutation DID take place, but it would have taken a fantastic coincidence for it to occur in my birdroom at exactly the same time as I was striving to achieve it. As far as the Budgerigars of other countries are concerned, I have visited the UK on many occasions and have always seen super Greys and Grey Greens. The masks and spots of Jim Moffat's best birds impress me. When good Budgerigars are mentioned the names of Harry Bryan, Mrs Angela Moss and Ormerod & Sadler always come to mind. However, I believe that in features such as feather quality, directional feathering, capping, the clear cap going further back, spot shape and fertility my Budgerigars are better than those of the past.

What is the best way of breeding a good Grey or Grey Green?

Gordon and Sylvia Hallam:

One cannot set out to breed a good one, all that one can do is to pair up the birds at one's disposal, trust that a fair percentage breed successfully and hope you breed something of quality. We never know from

This young Jo Mannes' Grey Green hen is typical of the soft-feathered Buff Budgerigars that he sets out to breed.

which pairs the best youngsters will appear. More often than not, the pairs upon which we place most hope fail to produce sufficient numbers to give them a sporting chance. Our system is simple. We select a particular Budgerigar; it may be a cock or it may be a hen, and select a number of partners that could be suitable. These are placed in show cages for evaluation. If the first bird chosen has a particular failing then we must find a partner which excels in the feature. If we are unable to find a suitable partner – or if we do not agree on the pairing – the original bird is put back in its cage or flight, for another day. We take a long time pairing up Budgerigars. Time taken at this stage can make or break a breeding season. It is amazing how often one of us thinks that they have found a good pair only for the other to find a reason for not making it. We believe that this is why man/wife partnerships have a distinct advantage. We have followed

Gordon and Sylvia Hallam pause for a moment as they go about their birdroom tasks. Since retiring, they are able to take a more leisurely approach. (photograph: Les Lockey)

Bernard Kellett has also retired, in his case from being a lecturer in Economics. He can now take more time over his morning nest-box inspections. (photograph: Les Lockey)

This young Grey cock, bred by Bernard Kellett, is already showing great promise. (photograph: Les Lockey)

A well-ordered sink unit and shelf. Bernard Kellett uses the shelf as a judging trestle when assessing and training his Budgerigars for the show bench. (photograph: Les Lockey)

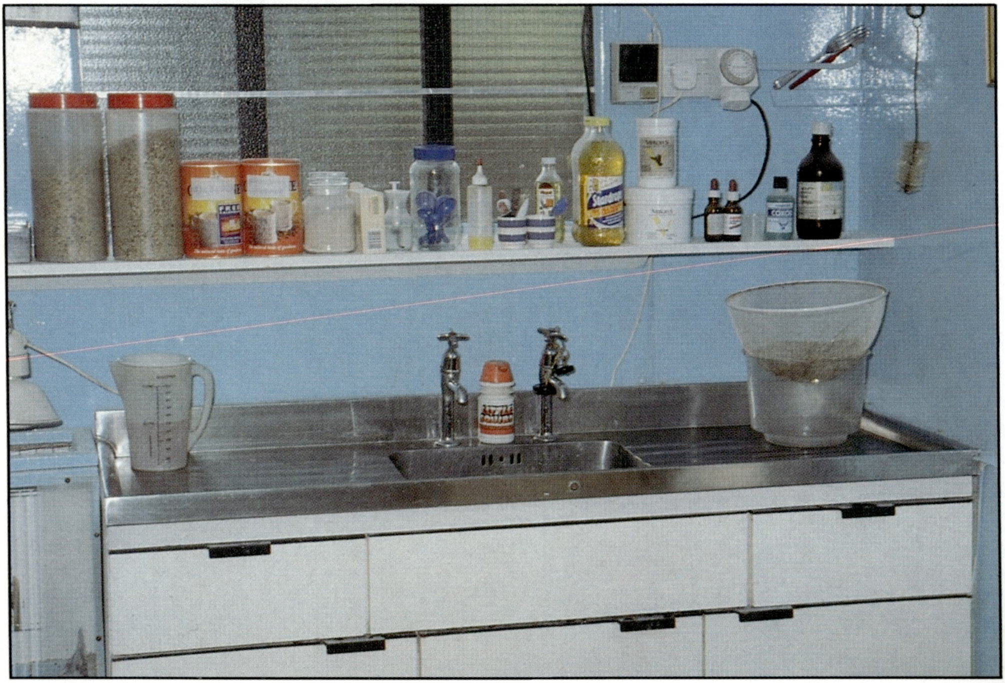

The pose of this Punchard Grey Green cock reveals its excellent width of head and powerful shoulders. (photograph: Les Lockey)

You could be forgiven for thinking that these are two photographs of the same bird. They are, in fact, two different Grey Greens that demonstrate the excellence of the Mannes stud. (photographs: Les Lockey)

Gordon and Sylvia Hallam are renowned for the quality of their hens. This super Grey Green reveals why. (photograph: Les Lockey)

Although not yet prepared for showing, this Grey cock from the Hallam stud shows real quality. (photograph: Les Lockey)

Another powerful Grey cock which exudes quality. This one was bred by Frank and John Punchard. (photograph: Les Lockey)

For roundness and expression, this Kellett Grey Green cock takes some beating. (photograph: Les Lockey)

Two lovely Grey hens. The one on the left was bred by Gordon and Sylvia Hallam. The one below was bred by Jo Mannes. (photographs: Les Lockey)

A super Grey Green cock; typical of the many winners produced by the Punchard stud. (photograph: Les Lockey)

This outstanding young Grey hen, bred by Les Lockey, proves that he is not only the top photographer of Budgerigars; he also produces birds that can beat the best. (photograph: Les Lockey)

Yet another excellent Grey Green from the Punchard stud. This youngster is brimming with potential. (photograph: Les Lockey)

This Grey Green hen has taken several top awards for Jo Mannes, including best opposite sex in show at the 1993 European championship, staged at Karlsruhe. (photograph: Les Lockey)

The type of Grey cock that demonstrates why so many breeders, the world over, want to acquire "Mannes' feather". (photograph: Les Lockey)

this system for 20 years and it has paid off. If the birds are always correctly balanced visually, year after year, you can be sure that any fault displayed by a particular bird is not inbred. Many a time, a visually poor Budgerigar, paired with an outstanding specimen, has produced youngsters of outstanding quality. If you follow our system and occasionally use inferior Budgerigars, you must use partners of the highest quality in order to compensate for the poor bird's failings. A word of warning! This system will only work if the poor Budgerigars have been bred from quality birds from an established stud of quality. Following the selection of a pair, we check their pedigrees. Unless they are brother and sister or parent and offspring, we carry on with the pairing. We never look at pedigrees before selecting pairs in case the paperwork unduly affects the final decision. It is important to breed reasonable quantities of youngsters but some breeders are over-optimistic. We have a quick rule of thumb: if 50 per cent of the pairs are successful, you are doing well; if 50 per cent of the eggs laid are fertile, you are doing well; if 50 per cent of the fertile eggs produce perching chicks, you are doing well. In order that the maximum use is made of breeding cages, it is important that plenty of spare birds are retained; both to give more choice when pairing up and to replace unsuccessful pairs. If 50 per cent of 40 pairs are successful you are, effectively, producing from 20 pairs. If you replace the 20 unsuccessful pairs and 50 per cent of these succeed, you are producing from 30 pairs. One step further and you have 35 pairs producing youngsters.

Bernard Kellett:

I realised early on that no matter how good or well-bred a pair of Budgerigars might be, what really mattered was how well they "clicked" as a pair. So it is important to know the background of each bird and to consult one's memory or records as to the results of previous pairings with the same background. Eventually, one can almost predict what type of Budgerigars a given pair will produce, although the degree of excellence will owe quite a lot to good fortune. I am constantly aware of the danger of regression and each pairing allows for this factor. For example, I do not pair a fine-feathered cock with a fine-feathered hen because I believe this would be a backward step; the quickest way of helping Nature to reclaim its own. My favourite pairings for producing good Grey Greens are: Normal Grey Green x Normal Light Green, Normal Grey Green cock x Opaline Grey Green hen and Normal Grey Green cock x Opaline Light Green hen. If I have a cock which is not a Grey Green I always pair it with a hen capable of producing Grey Green youngsters. For example, a Normal Blue, Grey or Green cock is paired with a Normal or Opaline Grey Green hen. Obviously, the physical characteristics and feathering of each bird is a major consideration when choosing pairings. I seldom use Opaline x Opaline, largely because Opaline cocks have little appeal for me. Because of marking problems, Opalines tend not to do well on the show bench. That is not to say I would not use an exceptional Opaline or Cinnamon cock in my breeding programme. I would pair it with a Normal hen to produce Normal split cocks and these would be paired with Normal hens to produce Normal cocks. My favourite pairing is a Normal Grey Green cock with excellent facial characteristics, good backskull and a powerful body mated to an Opaline hen which has a deep mask, style and a long body. I have found that big-faced cocks tend to produce cobby youngsters unless paired with long-bodied hens. Nowadays, I never pair two flecked-headed Budgerigars together because this leads to a build-up of flecking in the genetical background of the stud. In the past, many of my pairings have been based on a balancing-up process but, as time goes by, I am able to adopt a policy of doubling-up on good points. The former policy helps to maintain a certain standard, although it runs the risk of regression if the balancing factor works contrary to one's expectations. On the other hand, doubling-up has the promise of improvement and the possibility of producing youngsters which are better than their parents. I firmly believe in pairing related Budgerigars. I have tried all the variations but the ones which have been most successful have been: half-brother x half-sister, cousin x cousin and grandfather x granddaughter (or vice-versa). Although father x daughter is often a failure I have used it with success when the father has been an unrelated outcross. Indeed, this is a good way of assessing the quality of a newly-introduced bloodline.

Frank and John Punchard:

Even before one breeding season starts, you should be thinking about the next. Pairings should be selected not just to produce show winners but also to breed stock birds to advance the stud in future years. It is essential to consider a Budgerigar's pedigree as well as its physical appearance. If you can remember the appearance of its ancestors you will be able to take into account their weaknesses and strengths. Armed with all the available information, we can start selecting pairings – a process that often starts before the previous breeding season has finished. Pedigree plays such an important part in our decisions that our pairings are usually made on paper, without ever putting the partners together. The ability to carry a picture of each bird in our minds' eye is a big advantage. If you cannot do this you should assess proposed partners together. We start with the best six cocks and check through the pedigrees of the hens until each has a suitable mate. Because we keep more hens than cocks, there is still a good selection to choose from when we come to the last pairings. It is not unusual for two or three pairings to have the same pedigree background. Since the object is to breed Normals we work to certain rules. Two Budgerigars of the same sex-linked mutation are never paired together. A non-Normal cock is always paired with a Normal hen. Any split cocks are paired with Normal hens. We do not like to pair a split cock with a hen of the variety that is being carried by the cock, but will do so if the pairing looks ideal. These rules permit us to keep a check on split cocks. Normal hens are the backbone of our stud. We try to bring in one or two outcrosses each year and pair them to the best birds. Although the youngsters produced are not always what we hope for, they can produce the desired effects when paired back with our own lines. Close breeding fixes bad points as well as god ones and so there is no point in inbreeding unless the Budgerigars concerned are of top quality. We both inbreed with our favourite pairings being half-brother to half-sister, cousin to cousin and, sometimes, father to daughter. The idea is to breed Budgerigars whose good points are dominant when they are paired with Budgerigars that lack them.

Jo Mannes:

When I am selecting breeding pairs, I consider the feathering on three distinct parts of each bird; the head, mask and body. I sometimes remove a feather from prospective partners (making sure that they come from exactly the same place) so that I can compare them. My aim is to pair birds with contrasting feather types in order to produce the Budgerigars that have the feathering I want; wide, soft feathering on head and mask with shorter feathers on the body. Soft-feathered Buffs have more down beneath their feathers. It is seen easily on chicks as they feather up and can be detected on a mature bird when it is handled. This type of feathering around the vent can be a barrier to fertilisation and so I pull the feathers from around the vents of both cocks and hens. I believe that pulling feathers is less disfiguring than cutting them, but it does mean that they have to be pulled again for the second round. Most of my big, Buff cocks are not used for breeding until they are 18 months old. They take a long time to mature and often breed even better when they are aged two. By contrast hens with the feather texture that I call "super-Buff" are paired when they are eight or nine months old. They are always difficult to breed from but I have found it best to pair them early. Once this type of hen reaches two years of age they are usually finished as far as breeding is concerned. When super-Buff hens DO breed they often produce very good chicks and so I do not exhibit them; preferring to persist in trying to get them to breed. I always keep the best of the middle-Buff hens as they breed well, but I do not pair them until they are a little older. Although I try to breed from super-Buffs, there is a lot to be said for middle-Buffs. While you are producing three chicks from a super-Buff you might well breed 15 from its middle-Buff brother and, from a quality stud, the more you breed the more chance there is of producing an outstanding specimen. An interesting statistic is that, over the years, the best youngsters have tended to come from the first and third breeding rounds. Although quality, rather than colour, is always my main consideration, colour and variety have to come into the reckoning at some point. I do not like to pair two Budgerigars together that both carry the Grey factor. A Grey Green x Grey pairing, for example, produces too much feather and too many double-factor Greys and Grey Greens. In my experience, the best pairings for Greys and Grey Greens involve Blues. Grey Green/Blue x Skyblue has produced some super Grey Greens and Greys for me and Grey x Skyblue is the best pairing for producing top-quality Greys. Grey/Blue x

Dark Green/Blue pairings have given me some super Cobalts and Dark Greens. One reason for my preference for pairing different colours together is that same x same pairings tend to increase opalescence; undesirable body colour showing on the neck and/or wings. The Opaline factor is also associated with head flecking but occasionally it is worth pairing a flecked Opaline hen with a small-spotted cock to improve spot size. This is the only reason for using a flecked Opaline. Breeding with Buff Budgerigars can lead to some loss of body colour. This has been noticeable in many studs from the past. I have overcome the problem by using Dark-factor birds. This has been no hardship because I have liked Cobalts, Violets and Dark Greens ever since I took up Budgerigars. I have found that chicks with one Dark-factor parent consistently display better coloration, even when they, themselves, are of a Light shade. Greens, Blues, Spangles (for colour brightness), Opaline hens (for shoulder and spots) and Dark-factor birds are all useful in breeding good Greys and Grey Greens. Having a large stud permits me to keep Budgerigars in families without pairing too closely. The closest I breed is cousin x cousin and uncle x niece. I have not found father x daughter to be a beneficial pairing. Even better than pairing relations directly is a breeding plan that spans several generations. For example, starting with two particularly good chicks from the same nest (say two cocks), I pair one of them to a suitable unrelated, or distantly-related mate. The chicks from this mating are used for breeding the following year to produce the "grandchildren" generation. The best of the granddaughters is then paired back to her grandfather's brother. I have found this final pairing to be wonderfully successful.

How would you advise a newcomer to Greys and Grey Greens to set up a successful stud?

Gordon and Sylvia Hallam:

Our advice is to get around as many big shows as possible and to study as many Budgerigars as possible – and take your time! Time spent looking around will be repaid many times over. The old saying: "Act in haste and repent at leisure", is very apt. Try to understand why a judge came to his decision. If you are drawn to a particular fancier's birds, study his entire show team and see if they all have the same look. Hopefully you will be attracted to one or two studs; then visit those studs. When you visit a stud, keep your eyes open, your ears open and your mouth shut – except to ask questions. There is so much to take in that any time you spend talking is wasted. Try to assess the average quality of the stud. The higher that average is, the better. Look in all of the out-of-the-way cages, look for the health and happiness of the birds. If needs be, make a note of questions that you would like to ask. Most fanciers are a mine of information. Eventually you will have to make up your mind. And when you do, we suggest that you decide how much you want to spend on your initial stock. Then buy as many pairs of current-year-bred birds as you can afford. Buy the cheapest Budgerigars available. Do not be tempted to spend a lot on any one Budgerigar at this stage. Pair the birds as best you can, avoiding doubling up on faults. Be prepared to compromise as the object is to breed as many youngsters as you can, to increase your choice. Poor quality Budgerigars tend to breed prolifically. Certainly, the better the Budgerigars the poorer the breeding results tend to be. Hopefully, after the breeding season you will have a good selection to choose from. If you picked the right stud to buy from you should have a number of youngsters that are better than the birds you bought. Remember that they are young birds when you compare them with their mature parents. Retain all birds that are better than their parents and, depending upon numbers, you may need to keep some of the poorer hens. Make note of which of the original birds produced the best youngsters. Even at this early stage, assess your stud for its weaknesses. When you find one – say shortness in mask – go back to the original breeder and tell him that you wish to buy a Budgerigar or two which excel in depth of mask. You may have to pay more than previously. The new acquisitions should be paired with the best youngsters, but you now have to work at your pairings. You can get away with "lucky dip" for one year, but not two. It could be worth cross-pairing the original birds to find out if any of them are prepotent for producing better than themselves. Size is important, but not ALL important. No matter who you are you will not breed all big Budgerigars, but if they a carrying genes for size and are well fed you will breed a proportion of large Budgerigars. Do not be tempted to sell very high quality small Budgerigars. Paired with longer birds they may well produce exhibition quality stock. If you see an improvement each year, you should carry on buying the odd selected bird from your original supplier. If not, look elsewhere for your annual "top-up" purchases. Do not be put off by other people's comments about fanciers and their prices. Check them out for yourself.

Bernard Kellett:

When setting up a stud the first consideration – obviously – has to be the amount of cash available. Assuming that this is somewhat limited, I would hold back from making any purchases until many shows and aviaries have been visited. By the end of this period I would have gained knowledge of who are the successful breeders – and the prices they charge. Good Budgerigars are scarce and this is reflected in price, but some of the prices being charged today far exceed the value of the birds being sold. Part of the trouble is that beginners tend to measure quality by the price being asked. I would seek out a champion with a reputation for fair dealing. I would tell him how much I had to spend and then, if at all possible, purchase young birds. Initially, I would be more concerned with quality than colour but, after a couple of years, if I decided to specialise I would prune the stock accordingly. If money is a problem it is a good idea to retain a couple of brightly-coloured pairs so that their chicks could be sold as pets to help

"A good Grey Green is a joy to behold", says Bernard Kellett. He bred this young hen to prove the point.

cover the cost of seed. I would invite the original breeder to look at my developing stud and ask for advice about the next stage and possible purchases. Depending upon how quickly your "eye for a bird" develops, you will eventually be able to make your own decisions. In the case of Grey Greens I would always try to use a Normal cock in each pairing. From the initial pairings I would select and breed from the best youngsters from each pair thereby establishing families. Never be tempted to sell the better youngsters because these may well represent your future in the Fancy. By visiting your initial champion over a period, you will learn which are his better families and it may be possible to purchase birds from the lower end of these lines. The value of buying from a champion with an established stud is that he will have spent years breeding out faults, whereas a less experienced fancier will not. Avoid like the plague those fanciers who have collections rather than studs. The most important skill to develop is selecting the best possible pairings. Much will depend upon luck but a lot of so-called luck is the result of deep thought and sound management.

Frank and John Punchard:

The first thing a newcomer must learn is to be patient. Ideally, he would build an aviary with a supply of electricity. While the building is going on he should join a specialist Budgerigar club which holds regular meetings. He will meet fellow fanciers, make friends, learn about the Fancy and begin to appreciate what an exhibition Budgerigar should look like. He should view as many Budgerigars as possible, make notes of who is winning in young bird classes at larger shows and build up a profile of the hobby. Only then should he think about buying birds. Very low-priced Budgerigars should be purchased, to gain experience in the first year. In spite of the low price, the first Budgerigars should come from good lines so that they are capable of producing better than themselves. If he is not sure about the quality of the birds he breeds in the first season he should either exhibit them or ask an experienced fancier for advice. The advice might be hurtful, but it may put him on the right road. He can visit a breeder whose birds he admires. Two or three matched pairs from this source should form the basis of a sound stud. Alternatively, he could visit two breeders and start with four or six pairs. At this stage colour and variety should not be taken into consideration, but it is important to be prepared to refuse birds if they are not of the standard required. It is not unusual for a breeder to let Cinnamons or Opalines go which are of a higher quality than the Normals he is prepared to sell, so it is better to leave specialisation until later. With a bit of luck, the pairs will produce chicks and it may be possible to see that one breeder's stock has produced better than the other. If so the next move is obvious, the newcomer should return to purchase birds that are a little better than those previously bought. Further visits to other fanciers should be continued and if a useful bird is offered it should be bought; remembering that some will knit into the original stock while others will not.

Jo Mannes:

If I had to start again I would visit as many shows as I could and study the exhibits carefully. I would make notes of who was exhibiting the sort of Budgerigars that I like; what I call "charming" birds. If the fancier had been winning for two or three years and if people who had bought birds from him were also doing well, I would try to buy stock from him. Starting with only two or three pairs would take too long to establish a stud. Success will come much more quickly if you can obtain as many as 20 pairs. It is important to remember that you would not just be acquiring 40 Budgerigars; you would be buying the fruits of 10 years work. The stock would have to be related, have good shoulders, masks and spots. Feather is important. I would want soft-feathered Budgerigars. A quick guide is the shape of the mask spots. Round spots on a Buff Budgerigar indicate soft feathering, whereas elongated spots indicate hard feathering. Later, when experience has been gained, it will be possible to distinguish between hard and soft feathering by handling a bird. I would be looking for stock birds rather than show birds. Many good show birds do not breed and so I would try to buy their brothers and sisters. The smaller nest-mates of the winners can produce stock that are worth working with. They cost much less and breed to a much greater age. In general it is best to buy young birds, but you have to listen to experienced fanciers. Older Budgerigars can and do produce excellent youngsters but you have to be able to trust the seller. If offered older birds, look the seller in the eye and ask whether it has bred well, recently. Ask yourself why he has kept a three-year-old bird for so long. If it had been no good he would have got rid of it when it was younger. You need a bit of luck because there will always be an element of risk when buying livestock.

How important is it for you to ring chicks at the earliest possible time?

Gordon and Sylvia Hallam:

Like everyone else, we like to have breeder rings on youngsters - BUT - the most important thing is to breed chicks. We have found that November is not the best time to pair up for a good breeding season. September onwards is better. In the final analysis, it depends when the birds moult.

Bernard Kellett:

I am one of the growing group of fanciers who are ignoring the need to pair up in late-November so that their first chicks are ringed with the next year's rings. I prefer to start operations around the end of September when the birds seem to be fitter to breed. There is time to assess the results of parents and to make changes. The second round chicks are available for the show season and their parents are well-rested before being shown.

Frank and John Punchard:

Most breeders in the UK pair up their Budgerigars in November, which means that most of the chicks will wear the new year's rings. However, the main criterion must be the fitness of the birds. It is nice to have good chicks hatched before April so that they can compete from the start of the show season but, if that is not possible, there is always another show season and quality always shines through.

Jo Mannes:

The ring issue date in Germany is November 1, but I would like it to be a month earlier because many of my Budgerigars are ready and fit to breed in September. Some of today's modern Budgerigars have to be paired when they want to breed. In any case, I always like to have a few chicks in the nest and so keep five or six pairs breeding the whole year round.

How do you go about acquiring stock of the required quality?

Gordon and Sylvia Hallam:

We never have any problems obtaining outcrosses. Our strategy is quite simple. We are active members of our local Budgerigar society and always go on the club's aviary visits. If we are impressed by a particular stud we usually ask if there is a sales cage. Most breeders have such a cage, with Budgerigars usually at very reasonable prices. If a Budgerigar catches our eye, we make enquiries and if the ancestry sounds interesting we will probably buy it. We nearly always buy young Budgerigars. We never buy top quality, preferring to look for small, typey birds. We pair these to our very best.

Bernard Kellett:

Obtaining outcrosses of the desired quality is never easy for champion breeders, particularly for those who have done some winning. Buying a really good Normal Grey Green is extremely difficult and costly and so I have had to resort to the odd purchase of Opalines, Cinnamons and, more recently, Spangles in order to introduce new blood. Exchanges can be fruitful but, with a small stud, there is the danger of losing a Budgerigar of known quality in exchange for one whose breeding potential is unknown. Fortunately, because I have a circle of friends with related stock, the problem is minimised.

Frank and John Punchard:

No-one in their right mind is going to sell their best Budgerigars unless offered a ludicrously high price. That disqualifies all but the very rich. So this leaves purchasing the bits that make a good Budgerigar and fitting them together like a jigsaw puzzle. We prefer exchanging birds, which means letting a very good Budgerigar go – for which we expect a very good Budgerigar in return. It is no good to either party if the birds are inferior. We are always looking out for Budgerigars that would help our stud. We usually see them on the show bench and check the rest of the exhibitor's show team. If these are not of a similar standard we leave it at that. If we are pleased with what we see we arrange to visit the exhibitor, look at the stud and take things from there. In practice, the Budgerigars that interest us are usually owned by fanciers whose studs we know well.

Jo Mannes:

I used to exchange birds but without much success. Now, I have such a large stud, incorporating many different families, that I hope I will not need to bring in new birds. It is conceivable that there might be a feature which I would like to bring in, but what about the problems I could also be importing? I prefer to operate on the "closed-flock" principle.

Do you ever sell the best Greys and Grey Greens from your stud?

Gordon and Sylvia Hallam:

We are occasionally prepared to part with better adult birds, as long as we have bred something from them and have show team replacements. We do not sell top quality young birds. They are the future of the stud. It is important not to part with any bird just because you receive a good offer.

Bernard Kellett:

In my judgement, my best birds are the are those which have bred or have the potential to breed quality stock; particularly those dominant birds which breed better than themselves. I have only once sold one of these and that was after it had given me two breeding seasons.

Frank and John Punchard:

We never sell our best Budgerigars until we have bred from them and then, if they leave, it is to be exchanged. Selling your best birds is the shortest route to disaster. If one of our best birds bred better than itself, we would sell it because it would have no further place in our breeding plans.

Jo Mannes:

In general, the very best Budgerigars do not leave the stud until have bred well for me for two seasons. An exception is when an outstanding bird has been paired with two mates and the quality of both sets of chicks has been disappointing. I do sell top-quality Budgerigars, but only after I have used them for breeding and have better ones to retain. I keep a computer record of all of the birds I sell (and all of my breeding records). This enables me to keep track of who has birds from particular families.

What, in your opinion, is the degree of difficulty of Greys and Grey Greens?

Gordon and Sylvia Hallam:

We believe that breeding winners in the Grey and Grey Green colour series is neither easier nor harder than breeding winners in any of the other colours. The birds are naturally of a dominant variety and to breed birds of a set standard is easier - but then the competition on the show bench is much more competitive.

Bernard Kellett:

A major difficulty for the breeder of Grey Greens is the degree of opposition he faces on the show bench. Every year many outstanding specimens are bred. While this does not concern me too much, it could affect newcomers seeking success at shows. Another problem is that Grey Greens often produce other colours and sometimes their quality can exceed the quality of the Grey Greens themselves. So it is easy to be sidetracked from specialising in Grey Greens. To some extent this has happened to me, with Cinnamons. Nowadays I keep the two lines apart as much as possible. Perhaps the major difficulty is maintaining quality over a long period, coupled with the need to breed better Budgerigars each year.

Frank and John Punchard:

As far as colour is concerned, Greys and Grey Greens are one of the easiest to produce because the Grey factor is dominant. The difficulty is in breeding good specimens. Because the competition is the strongest, you have to breed one that has that little bit extra if it is to win consistently but, whereas the best examples of some varieties can pick up regular challenge certificates and never challenge for the top awards, a winning Grey or Grey

Green is seldom out of the reckoning for the specials. It is a challenge to produce specimens regularly that can compete with the best and so Greys and Grey Greens are not for the faint hearted.

Jo Mannes:

Grey and Grey Greens are not especially difficult to breed to the highest exhibition standards.

Are there any tactics that can help you win with Greys and Grey Greens?

Gordon and Sylvia Hallam:

It takes hard work to make a good specimen a winner - and good luck. Many super Budgerigars never see the show bench because they are are always short of a tail or a spot and, in that condition, there is little you can do to get them on the show bench. Many fanciers completely de-spot a Budgerigar several weeks before a show to try to ensure it will have a full complement when the time comes. But even that does not always work. We

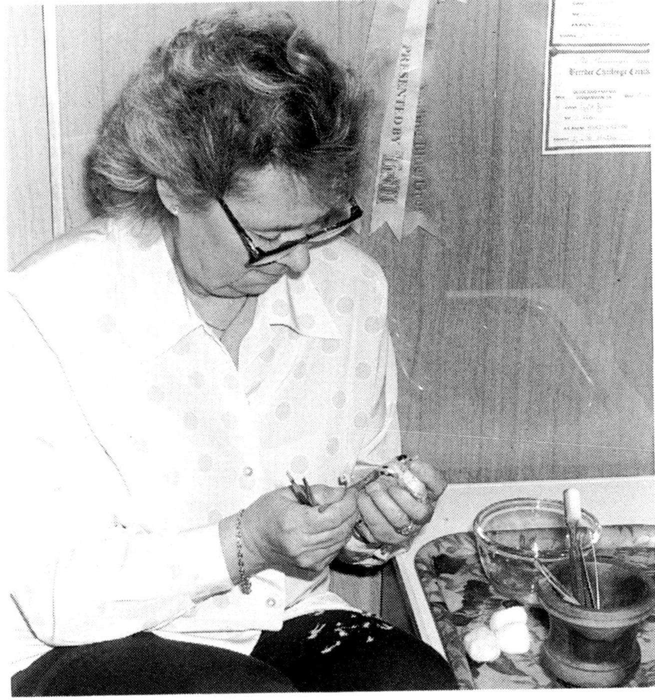

Sylvia Hallam is well-equipped to practice her skill at show preparation.

once waited eight weeks for a spot to regrow. Pulling tails is even more hazardous; sometimes they never return. We rarely pull tails, but if we do we pull one first and wait to see that it is regrowing before pulling the other. The hard work element encompasses both the preparation of the birds and maintenance of show cages. Some may scorn the trouble we go to but, very often, little separates a Budgerigar that comes second in its class and the winner of the best in show award. Anything that could swing the decision in your favour should be done. The judge might think that the exhibitor who puts his Budgerigar out in a clean cage has tried harder and deserves to be rewarded. Any well-conditioned Budgerigar in a clean cage is a credit and a good advertisement to any owner. A dirty cage could be a health hazard to other Budgerigars and fanciers and, as such, should be heavily penalised. If that happened we would soon see an improvement in general presentation.

Bernard Kellett:

Always remember that a judge is just as concerned with faults as good points. A Budgerigar can win by default; not only because of its own excellence but because its rivals have faults. In other words, one tactic is to leave a Budgerigar with obvious faults at home. What is the point of risking a Budgerigar's well-being by taking it to a show when it has no chance of winning? Spraying, discussed earlier, is important as is the treatment of mask and spots. A badly spotted-out Budgerigar is indicative of a careless fancier and, in a sense, is an insult to the judge. A keen-eyed judge will soon spot faults of tails and flights so these need attention. Showmanship is often inherited, but show cage training does help, particularly if a bird is going to be handled roughly by a steward on its way to being judged. Washing and brushing the feathers above the cere and around the beak can improve a Budgerigar's appearance greatly. Frontal rise is enhanced, beak and eyes become less visible and that desirable, eye-catching, "pussy-cat" appearance is evident. Ideally, I would enter three or four birds in each class but, in practice, this is reduced by a whole series of mishaps, common to all fanciers. I positively refuse to take Budgerigars to shows unless they have a chance of being placed which means that, very frequently, my show entry is greatly depleted.

Frank and John Punchard:

There is no easy way of making a good Budgerigar a winner. A showman is born and, no matter how hard you try, you cannot teach "swank" or charisma. What you can do is turn out a bird in optimum condition; 100 per cent fit, no extra flecks of spot left in the mask, tail and flight feathers not ragged and clean - particularly around the beak and cap. First impressions carry a lot of weight and judges tend to register head qualities first. Judges are there to judge Budgerigars, but a good show cage CAN make a difference. A good Budgerigar deserves a good cage. Our normal Grey and Grey Green show team would ideally consist of three young cocks, two young hens and two adult cocks. We seldom show adult hens. In practice, how many we exhibit depends upon their quality and whether they are show fit. There is no point in benching a bird that has no chance of winning. Our total show team usually numbers 18 to 24 exhibits with the rest being made up mainly of Light Greens and Normal Cinnamons.

Jo Mannes:

To win, Budgerigars need to be staged to perfection. I do not spray my show team a great deal but prefer to wash their heads and masks before a show. A good show Budgerigar obviously enjoys being in a show cage. Even at the top German shows I enter only one bird in each class. I choose the one I think is best and then show it.

How do you go about judging Greys and Grey Greens?

Gordon and Sylvia Hallam:

Although we choose not to judge, that does not stop us from having views about judges and judging. As far as Grey Greens are concerned, most judges are fairly competent. It really depends upon their personal preferences. If a judge must have large spots, and your Budgerigar has small ones, you're in trouble. When we enter several Budgerigars in the same class we know which one we like best but can never be sure which the judge will go for. A judge, in a moment of insanity, might place your poorer bird first, thus preventing your best bird from going any further. On the other hand, you will have won the class. Even when a Budgerigar has won under a particular judge, it is not guaranteed to do the same next time he adjudicates upon it. Condition might change and the competition changes constantly. It has even been suggested that some judges knock back Budgerigars that have won under them previously – and so it goes on. In general terms, a good judge is one under whom you do well. In other words, they like the same type of Budgerigars that you do.

Bernard Kellett:

My first tactic is to stand well back from the judging trestle to gain a comparative view of all the entries. I then place the best Budgerigar to the far left and progressively rank the rest. Birds with no chance of being placed are quickly removed from the scene, thereby reducing the numbers to be judged. Only then do I start to make a close scrutiny of each individual's good and bad points. What I am looking for is an approximation to the characteristics of the "Ideal". Such factors as size, head qualities, depth of mask, spot size and shape are all considered. With the Grey Green I am also keen on the quality of colour which I like to be vibrant. It is the intermediate and coarse-feathered Budgerigars which are most attractive to me because they convey the principle of the power bird which is currently in vogue. Grey Greens are usually good example of this type of Budgerigar. Accordingly, the poorer birds – those that are sleek, narrow-shouldered, tight-masked, small and particularly those with large beaks and protruding eyes – are marked down. One major problem is the super bird which has a missing tail or flight feathers. Should the gap in quality between that and its nearest rival be great, I would choose it even though the rival was feather perfect. This can upset some fanciers who are quick to point out the faults of the winner while ignoring the vast difference in quality. Judges give opinions and these – like fanciers – differ greatly in spite of the Budgerigar Society's scale of points which, incidentally, I am perfectly happy with. A judge does not know that a given Budgerigar can be a show-stopper on its day. All a judge can base his judgement on is how the bird performs for the few minutes it is before him. Because I understand the difficulties which face judges I have no problem in accepting other judges' verdicts. However, that does not stop me believing that some judges who specialise in the rarer varieties tend to be a little harsh on Grey Greens, particularly when they are coarse-feathered or carrying a little ticking. But it really is a case of swings and roundabouts and, in general, I am only too happy that someone has foregone the comfort of his own fireside, perhaps to travel a long distance, to consider the merits of my Budgerigars. Judges are too frequently the butt of frustrated and inconsiderate exhibitors.

Frank and John Punchard:

The first job is to check whether the birds are in the correct class and then, if there is time, give them a few minutes to settle down. For a class of up to 20, a glance along the line reveals if any birds stand out and these are moved to the head of the class (usually top left) but in no particular order. Any exhibits that are totally unfit, heavily flecked or with both main tail feathers missing are sent back to the staging. Those of lower quality are moved to the bottom rail of the judging trestle. The class is then judged, beginning with the birds we liked at first sight. Comparison continues until we have what appear to be the top eight or nine birds. The rest are then compared with the one in lowest place. If they are not up to standard they are returned to the staging. Assessment of finer points may result in some adjustment of positions. Before marking the cages we take a step back and assess the class as a whole. If the entry is greater than 20 we divide the class into two and judge it as two classes before combining them for the final assessment. Both of us consider head and mask qualities to be of prime importance, followed by deportment. The major colour fault of Normals is opalescence around the neck. It is not important for us to show under judges who keep Greys and Grey Greens. Which features a judge puts most

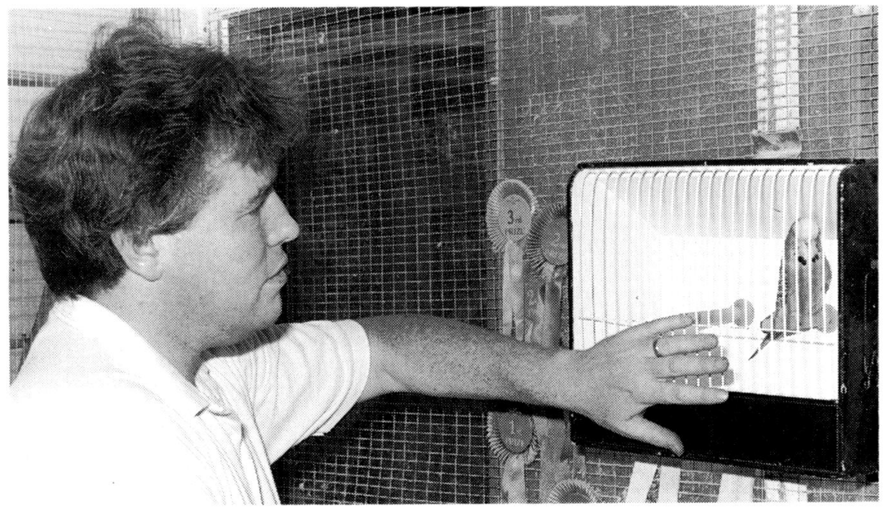

John Punchard studies an outstanding Grey Green cock.

emphasis on is more important. Some judges do not like the type of Budgerigars we keep and so we are not surprised when our birds lose. It is up to us to get to know a judge's preferences and put out the type he likes – if we have them. On numerous occasions we have left good Budgerigars at home because of who was judging. If we knew that all of the judges disliked our type of birds, John would keep the birds at home but Frank would carry on and show them. The Budgerigar Society's scale of points is heavily weighted in favour of size, shape, deportment, head and mask (80 out of 100) which is fine for Normals but discriminates against other varieties whose unique features are lost within the points total. Frank believes that the Scale of Points should be scrapped, with the written standard of excellence for each variety and the pictorial standard being a judge's only guide. John believes that the Scale of Points serves a useful purpose but that some adjustment is necessary to give proper recognition of the special features of each variety. The standards for Greys and Grey Greens are good, but some confusion arises from there being three shades; light, medium and dark. It would be useful if colour plates were issued to provide clarification.

Jo Mannes:

Condition is vital. In Germany a Budgerigar MUST have two long tail feathers. If more than two wing flights are missing an exhibit is heavily penalised. When judging I am looking for a the "good" Budgerigar I described at length in answer to the question: "What makes a good Grey or Grey Green?" Although most judges keep Greys and Grey Greens, some seem able to judge them better than others. There are judges who do not seem able to recognise the value of the best features of top-quality Budgerigars. Although there are differences in detail between German and UK standards, (for example, the ideal length in Germany is 9½in (24.1cm), while in the UK it is 8½in (21.6cm)) most judges are looking for the same type of Budgerigars when selecting winners.

How do you see the future of Greys and Grey Greens?

Gordon and Sylvia Hallam:

We believe that the future of Grey and Grey Green Budgerigars is rosy. The genes that they have inherited and the expertise of many dedicated fanciers will keep them at the forefront of the Budgerigar Fancy for many years to come.

Bernard Kellett:

I am a little concerned that Grey Greens are being used to improve other colours, such as Light Greens and Blues. Far too few fanciers are keeping Grey Greens for their own sake. A similar thing happened to the Opaline and we all know how much that variety suffered. Accordingly, I would like to see more fanciers specialising in Grey Greens and that will be my principal future role in the Fancy. A good Grey Green is a joy to behold, largely because a good one conforms so closely to the "Ideal" and displays all the power and stance desired of the modern Budgerigar. Multi-coloured studs may have their advantages, but I feel sure that at least a degree of specialisation must lead to future generations of more knowledgeable and committed fanciers.

Frank and John Punchard:

Greys and Grey Greens are already at the top of the tree so their future seems to be assured – at least in the short term. Their real strength for posterity lies in how many good Grey and Grey Green studs there are around. If one or two decline the varieties will not suffer – which is more than can be said about some other varieties. Directional feathering to give a fuller cap and a silky finish on the body feathers would be a big advance. We are convinced that Greys and Grey Greens will maintain their position at number one in the Budgerigar world.

Jo Mannes:

Greys and Grey Greens are among the strongest of Budgerigar varieties. They are getting better and will continue to improve. Even so, both have some way to go before they reach the level of quality I want to see.

CHAPTER 7

COLOUR EXPECTATIONS

The subject of Budgerigar colour expectations could fill a book on its own – in fact it HAS filled a book and anyone who wants to delve deeper into the subject should read Taylor and Warner's *Genetics for Budgerigar Breeders.*

Understanding genetics CAN help when it comes to breeding good Budgerigars, but it must be stressed that many of the breeders who have bred the best Budgerigars in the world have had only a sketchy knowledge of the subject. So, if you find the subject difficult to understand you will be in good company, and should not worry unduly. However, if you have ever been surprised by the appearance of a Green, or even a Blue, in the nest of two Grey Greens, this chapter should help you to understand why.

The first fact that needs to be understood is that, in every case, there are TWO factors controlling every individual colour and variety. In this book, the letters used to denote these are not necessarily the ones that are used in serious text books. For the sake of the first example, a Grey factor is represented by the letter "R" and a non-Grey factor by "N". So double-factor Grey (DF) is "RR", a single-factor Grey (SF) is "RN" and any Budgerigar with no Grey factor is "NN". When two Budgerigars mate, each gives ONE of its colour factors to each chick. The possible combinations can be represented by a grid of four squares. So what happens when two single-factor Grey Budgerigars mate and each parent passes on one of its factors to each chick?

		Grey (SF)	
		R	N
Grey (SF)	R	RR	RN
	N	RN	NN

A quarter of the chicks will be "RR" (double-factor Greys), a half will be "RN" (single-factor Greys) and a quarter will be "NN" (non-Greys). Translated into colours, this means that two single-factor Greys paired together will produce Greys and Blues. Because Grey is dominant to non-

Grey, a Budgerigar possessing only one Grey factor will still look like a Grey. The double-factor and single-factor Greys will be indistinguishable visually and it is only by test-mating that their genetic make-up can be established.

The following grid demonstrates what happens when a single-factor Grey ("RN") is paired with a non-Grey ("NN"):

		Grey (SF)	
		R	N
Non-Grey	N	RN	NN
	N	RN	NN

Half of the chicks will be "RN" (single-factor Greys) and the rest will be "NN" (non-Greys).

Next, let us check an "NR" (single-factor Grey) x "RR" (double-factor Grey) mating.

		Grey (SF)	
		R	N
Grey (DF)	R	RR	RN
	R	RR	RN

All of the chicks will be Grey, equally divided between double and single-factor.

The same procedure will show that a double-factor Grey x double-factor Grey mating will produce all double-factor Greys, two non-Greys paired together will produce all non-Greys and a double-factor Grey paired with a non-Grey will produce all single-factor Greys.

In the same way that Grey is dominant to non-Grey, Green is dominant to Blue. If a Green factor is denoted by "G" and a Blue factor by "B" then a Green is "GG" and a Blue is "BB". A Budgerigar that carries one Green and one Blue factor "GB" is known as a Green split Blue (Green/Blue) and, visually, is no different to a Green "GG". The outcome of pairing two Green/Blues ("GB") together follows the same pattern as pairing two single-factor Greys.

		Green split Blue	
		G	B
Green split Blue	G	GG	GB
	B	GB	BB

A quarter of the chicks will be "GG" (Greens), a half will be "GB" (Green split Blue, like their parents) and a quarter will be "BB" – Blues! That is how Blue Budgerigars can be bred from two that look just like Greens.

As long as you remember that a Grey Green is a Green with a Grey factor added and a Grey is a Blue with a Grey factor added it is fairly easy to work out, in two stages, the outcome of all the pairing combinations of Greys, non-Greys, Greens and Blues.

In some of the other books in this series (eg *All About Green Budgerigars* and *All About Blue Budgerigars*) the effect of the Dark factor has been explained. However, where Greys and Grey Greens are concerned, this will only complicate the issue, particularly as it is not always possible to distinguish between their Light, Medium and Dark versions. The adventurous may wish to carry out their own investigation by denoting Light as "LL", Medium as "LD" and Dark as "DD".

For those who have no wish to calculate colour expectations, the following tables will prove useful.

TABLE 1: Pairings involving Greys and non-Greys.
(with theoretical percentage expectations)

Pairing*	Expectations (cocks and hens)
Grey (DF) × Grey (DF)	100% Grey (DF)
Grey (DF) × Grey (SF)	50% Grey (DF) 50% Grey (SF)
Grey (DF) × non-Grey	100% Grey (SF)
Grey (SF) × Grey (SF)	25% Grey (DF) 50% Grey (SF) 25% non-Grey
Grey (SF) × non-Grey	50% Grey (SF) 50% non-Grey
non-Grey × non-Grey	100% non-Grey

* *(It makes no difference which colour is the cock and which is the hen)*

TABLE 2: Pairings involving Greens and Blues
(with theoretical percentage expectations)

Pairing*	Expectations (cocks and hens)
Green × Green	100% Green
Green × Blue	100% Green/Blue
Green × Green/Blue	50% Green 50% Green/Blue
Green/Blue × Green/Blue	25% Green 50% Green/Blue 25% Blue
Green/Blue × Blue	50% Green/Blue 50% Blue
Blue × Blue	100% Blue

* *(It makes no difference which colour is the cock and which is the hen)*

TABLE 3: Pairings involving Light Greens, Dark Greens and Olives.
(*with theoretical percentage expectations*)

Pairing*	Expectations (cocks and hens)
Light Green × Light Green	100% Light Green
Light Green × Dark Green	50% Light Green
Light Green × Olive	50% Dark Green 100% Dark Green
Dark Green × Dark Green	25% Light Green 50% Dark Green 25% Olive
Dark Green × Olive	50% Dark Green 50% Olive
Olive × Olive	100% Olive

* *(It makes no difference which colour is the cock and which is the hen)*

Further copies of this book and details about others in the "All about ..." series can be obtained from:

F. Wright,
31 Redford Avenue,
Wallington,
Surrey, SM6 9DT.

Telephone or Fax:
081-647 6378

Ask for details of quantity and club discounts